JANET MELROSE &
SHERYL NORMANDEAU

*The Prairie Gardener's
Go-To for*

Pests &
Diseases

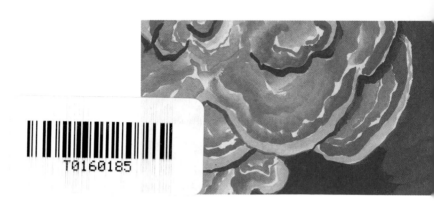

TOUCHWOOD

Copy edited by Paula Marchese

Design and Illustration by Tree Abraham

Photos by Janet Melrose and Sheryl Normandeau unless otherwise noted.

Photograph on p. 102 by Rob Normandeau. Used with permission.
Photograph on p. 105 by James Coleman/Shutterstock.com.
Photograph on p. 108 by Warren Metcalf/Shutterstock.com.
Photograph on p. 112 by Tina Boisvert. Used with permission.

LIBRARY AND ARCHIVES CANADA CATALOGUING IN PUBLICATION

Title: The Prairie gardener's go-to for pests and diseases / Janet Melrose and Sheryl Normandeau.
Names: Melrose, Janet, 1954- author. | Normandeau, Sheryl, author.
Description: Series statement: Guides for the Prairie gardener | Includes index.
Identifiers: Canadiana (print) 20190207280 | Canadiana (ebook) 20190207299 | ISBN 9781771513142 (softcover) | ISBN 9781771513159 (HTML)
Subjects: LCSH: Garden pests—Prairie Provinces. | LCSH: Plant diseases—Prairie Provinces. | LCSH: Weeds—Prairie Provinces. | LCSH: Garden pests—Control—Prairie Provinces. | LCSH: Phytopathogenic microorganisms—Control—Prairie Provinces. | LCSH: Weeds—Control—Prairie Provinces.
Classification: LCC SB603.5 M45 2020 | DDC 635/.04909712—dc23

TouchWood Editions gratefully acknowledges that the land on which we live and work is within the traditional territories of the Lkwungen (Esquimalt and Songhees), Malahat, Pacheedaht, Scia'new, T'Sou-ke and W̱SÁNEĆ (Pauquachin, Tsartlip, Tsawout, Tseycum) peoples.

We acknowledge the financial support of the Government of Canada and the Province of British Columbia through the Book Publishing Tax Credit.

This book was produced using FSC®-certified, acid-free papers, processed chlorine free, and printed with soya-based inks.

Printed in China

24 23 22 21 20   1 2 3 4 5

Dedicated to all prairie gardeners

Introduction 7

Introduction

*If you see this weird-looking critter, don't freak out! This is
a ladybug "teenager"—and this one is clearly planning to
decimate that population of aphids next to it.*

We strongly believe that we all have a responsibility to live (and garden!) with
regard and respect for the world around us. One of the easiest ways to do this is
to encourage biodiversity in our landscapes. That means increasing the richness
of species in your garden, which encompasses insects, birds, wildlife, and plants
of all kinds. Cultivate abundance and variety. Biodiverse spaces are habitats and
food sources for all living organisms, including humans.

Recognizing that all life is fully interconnected is the first step. Taking action to maintain biodiversity is the next. Avoid monocultures in your garden—planting only one genus or species often encourages insect and disease problems. Sustainability is a word that is sometimes tossed around in a cavalier manner nowadays, but there truly are concrete ways you can do your part to contribute to biodiversity. Conserve precious water resources, and strive to build healthy soil. Grow plants that pollinators and beneficial insects love, and make your garden a safe place for nesting and feeding birds and other visiting wildlife. Create compost from your garden and food wastes, and return it to the soil.

As our gardening philosophy focuses on the care and the health of all of the organisms in our little corners of the universe and beyond, you won't find us recommending that you should immediately reach for the spray bottles whenever a pest insect or disease threatens your plants. We advocate a strategy called Integrated Pest Management (IPM), with its multipronged approach of prevention, observation, identification, and, if necessary, control.

IPM was first introduced by American scientists and agricultural specialists in the late 1940s. A significant number of new synthetic pesticides were either available or under development at the time, and the concept of IPM was devised to ensure that these new products were used only when a commodity crop would be completely lost to pests—that is, when the economic risk tipped too far. According to the mandates of IPM, chemical controls would not be used unless the threat was severe, in order to minimize or prevent damage to the environment. Nowadays, we apply the principles of IPM to all types of pests, not just insects. Controls, if needed, are not merely chemical: They may also be organic, cultural, physical, or biological. The goal is to forgo controls unless absolutely required, and if there are options, use the control that has the smallest, least harmful impact on our ecosystems and the living creatures they contain.

It may seem ridiculously obvious, but a stress-free plant is healthier than one that is not growing under optimal conditions. From the moment we plant a seed, select a plant at the garden centre, or accept a rooted cutting from a friend, we are charged with providing the most hospitable environment we can for our plants to grow and thrive in. Everything is important: from siting and spacing and soil conditions to exposure to light and wind, and inputs of fertilizer and water. What you do is critical as well: You must keep up with weeding, deadheading, pruning, and mulching to take care of the life of the plant. You must also monitor your garden plants for early signs of insects or diseases and then determine if the problem is large enough to warrant action. Sometimes the issue is merely cosmetic; if that's the case, accept the blemishes and lumps and know that strong, healthy plants can usually cope with minor damage, especially if you are consistent with maintenance.

Of course, even if we make every attempt to encourage biodiversity in our gardens, and we work hard to keep our plants from exposure to stress, pests may still show up from time to time. If you notice that something isn't quite right in your garden, remember the tenets of IPM and accurately identify what you are dealing with. Once that task is accomplished, you can then decide if it's necessary to treat the problem. That's where this book comes in! We don't have room to take a look at all of the issues that might crop up in your prairie garden, but we examine many common plant problems and help you deal with them in the healthiest, most environmentally friendly way we can.

Let's get on with those questions!—SHERYL NORMANDEAU & JANET MELROSE

Weeds

1

Landscape fabric:
Should I use it as a weed barrier?

The short answer is no! Emphatically no!

Landscape fabric was originally developed for the agricultural industry for annual weed suppression. It was used seasonally and removed annually at the end of the growing year.

Somewhere along the way, it has been adopted into commercial and home garden use as a permanent means of weed suppression. We are all for using landscape fabric in situations where there is no intention to grow anything, such as under decks, pathways, and large rock installations where weed suppression is important, so as not to create a haven of weeds that are hard to get at and remove.

The attributes of good quality landscape fabric are said to include permeability when exposed to air and water and not being readily biodegradable in the soil.

However, despite these claims, using landscape fabric in the garden is not a permanent solution at all and usually leads to further problems that cause much more work to remediate. Here we speak from both personal experience and from tales told to us by other gardeners.

Despite the attributes of landscape fabric, it does, in fact, inhibit movement of air and water. It degrades over time, especially when exposed to sunlight. More importantly, underneath the fabric, the soil's quality is affected, as there is no chance to improve it with soil amendments and fertilizers. Soil life, including earthworms, is negatively impacted, and plant roots grow up into the fabric rather than deep into the soil. Overwintering insects are not able to nest or burrow through the fabric, leading to a loss of biodiversity. Furthermore, the fabric can girdle a tree, if not loosened, as the girth of the trunk increases over time.

Beyond all that, weeds do make a return; either they are carried on the wind or rain or they can literally grow up through the fabric, if the weeds are perennial in nature. In our windy, dry, and dusty summers, a fine sediment of soil builds up

There are better options than landscape fabric for weed suppression.

on top of the fabric, along with other organic matter, which creates an excellent growing medium for these pioneer species that we call weeds.

Gardens are constructed by us for pleasure and function and are always being disturbed, hence the perennial problem of weeds. Their job is to populate disturbed soil and work to improve it by mining it for nutrients, contributing their biomass over time, and, in many instances, improving the soil's texture with their taproots and rhizomes. We just prefer not to have them assisting us in our gardens and parks.

Reducing weeds in your garden can be better managed through cultural practices rather than a quick fix. Make improving your soil's structure, texture, and fertility a priority, so that the plants in your garden are healthy and grow well. Lay down organic mulches on a regular basis and renew as needed. Mulch will act as a barrier to weed seeds, as they will find it difficult to germinate in the mulch, and if they do grow, they are easy to remove. As the mulch degrades, it will continue the work of soil improvement. It doesn't take a lot of mulch to be effective, and the current trend to apply inches worth of mulch is not necessary.

Just a 1-inch (2.5-centimetre) layer will be sufficient, and will give all the benefits without excessive cost. Besides, we do want a bit of bare soil for our insects to be able to nest easily.

Mulch can be extra compost that is not incorporated into the soil, or wood chips, if your garden has a perennial bed. Annual gardens are better served with non-wood mulches, such as dried grass clippings, shredded paper, straw, burlap strips, or even large plant leaves such as rhubarb or comfrey.

Living mulches are another option for perennial beds. These are ground-covering species planted to cover bare soil with a creeping mat. Dense, low growing, and functional, these species provide the same benefit as other mulches. Creeping thyme, fairy bellflower (*Campanula persicifolia*), periwinkle, sweet woodruff, and hen and chicks are among the many species we can easily grow in prairie gardens.

The bottom line: Use landscape fabric only where there are to be no plants or leave it for the farmers to use, as it was intended originally.[1] —JM

Creeping bellflower: beautiful but nasty! Is there anything that I can do to eradicate it from my garden?

Creeping bellflower is gorgeous to look at, but it can quickly take over your whole garden.

Chances are you are familiar with it: creeping bellflower—the weed with the pretty blue flowers and the seriously insidious growth habit. To say creeping bellflower creeps is an understatement, at best—a more accurate word would be "stampedes." The gorgeous blooms are deceptively enticing, and many gardeners allow the plants to gain a foothold (stranglehold?) in their gardens, realizing belatedly that it was the wrong thing to do. (And it may be legally the wrong the thing to do—check the Weed Control Act of your province to determine if this plant must, by law, be eliminated in your yard.)

Creeping bellflower is a member of the genus *Campanula*, of which there are several commonly cultivated species that you can find in your local garden centre (and you may already be growing one or more of them in your garden). The bad one is *Campanula rapunculoides*. Don't ditch the others or yell at the garden centre staff, as the non-rapunculoides are companionable, pretty perennials that will add reliable colour to your garden.

Originally brought to North America as an ornamental from Europe, creeping bellflower grows up to forty inches (one metre) tall on strong stems that are not challenged by wind or poor weather. Creeping bellflower can grow in any soil type, and is adaptable to sun and part shade. It fares equally well in dry soils as well as wet. You can see where this is going: Creeping bellflower can grow pretty much anywhere, and it will — even going so far as extending its significant root system beneath sidewalks and patio stones.

Creeping bellflower reproduces in two ways, via rhizomatous root systems and when seeded. Each plant can produce a whopping 3,000 seeds annually, which can spell trouble for your garden and any others that the wind carries seed to.

The heart-shaped lower leaves of creeping bellflower are easy to spot in the spring, while the upper leaves are slender and lance-shaped. The flowers are borne above the leaves and are attractive to bees.

Hand-pulling is the best way to remove creeping bellflower from your garden, but it can be a relentlessly back-breaking, tedious, and ongoing task. If you leave a tiny chunk of root in the ground when you are weeding, a new plant will pop up. Dig deeply and horizontally, seeking the roots. Do not till the soil as this will just break up the roots and more plants will be reproduced. To prevent seeds from forming, remove the plants before they flower. Selective herbicides do not work well (or at all) on creeping bellflower. It is necessary to deal with it, plant by plant, one rhizome at a time. Try not to get too discouraged; know that you're not alone in your attempt to get rid of creeping bellflower. Most prairie gardeners are having the same problem.[2] — SN

Can I get rid of field horsetail on my property?

Field horsetail (*Equisetum arvense*) may be one of the more interesting plants on the prairies, but that doesn't mean everyone wants it in their garden.

This spore-producing plant loves consistently moist soil; you'll often spot it on the edges of bogs and other bodies of water, although it is also adaptable to other, drier conditions. Horsetail has two distinct stages of development. In early spring, the spore-bearing (fertile) stage is characterized by the emergence of a light brown stalk with highly visible segmented joints and a cone-like top. The fertile stalk has no leaves. The vegetative stalks immediately follow. These stems are extensively branched and look like fern leaves. They reach a height of approximately twenty inches (fifty centimetres).

Horsetail is capable of reproducing via spores and rhizomatous root systems that can dip 6 feet (1.8 metres) deep. Spores are produced in the thousands in early May and are carried by the wind.[3]

Horsetail is native to North America. It contains toxins that may be harmful to livestock, and it can be highly competitive (read: seriously aggressive) in its interactions with other plants. The best way to control the plants is by digging them up, as horsetail is largely resistant to selective herbicides. Removal of the fruiting parts isn't sufficient, as the plants will continue to reproduce underground. It is imperative to remove the entire root system to prevent the plants from starting up new growth from pieces of root. The rhizomes produce small tubers, which must also be removed. Tilling is not recommended if horsetail is present.[4] —SN

This fascinating plant can be troublesome in your garden, especially in damp soil.

Love 'em or hate 'em, dandelions are here to stay.

Dandelions: Give me options on what to do with this controversial plant!

Dandelions (*Taraxacum officinale*) need no introduction to prairie gardeners. This bold yellow bloom with the long branched taproot and a distinctive dark green rosette of lobed leaves is about as divisive as plants come—everyone, and I do mean *everyone*—has a strong opinion about what exactly to do with them. Some vehemently want to destroy them at all costs, while others praise them as significant bee (and human!) food. There is no denying their importance as a pollinator plant, and some gardeners deliberately cultivate them for that reason, as well as to bring them to the table in the form of raw and cooked greens, preserves, even beverages. Not everyone shares this viewpoint: If you're a soccer player, you're certainly not keen on dandelions tripping you up during an outdoor game, or if you're fond of a lush, pristine lawn, dandelions do not fit in with that objective. In the garden or agricultural field, dandelions may seriously outcompete cultivated crops.

If you're concerned about dandelions in your lawn, you can try to force them out by top-dressing your lawn and applying a native grass seed. Healthy lawns will discourage dandelions.[5] You could also try turfgrass alternatives, such as white clover, which will outcompete the dandelions (again, it's completely understandable that there may be gardeners out there who view clover in the same weedy category as dandelions, so this solution is not for everyone). Removing dandelions by manually pulling them is a recommended option. It is important to get as much of the taproot out as possible. For ease of pulling, perform the task after a rain. Mowing dandelions will also keep them from spreading, as long as you chop them down before the seed heads form and the winged pappi are released. Did you know that a single dandelion plant can produce up to 23,000 seeds?[6]—SN

Quackgrass or crabgrass: What is the difference and how can I control them?

When we see thick-bladed grasses growing much taller than the rest of the grass on our lawns, we often lump them together as one and the same, and try to control both with the same methods.

Digitaria, a genus of native and introduced wild grasses, is often called crabgrass for the way it looks like a crab with pinchers and legs growing in your lawn. The botanical name *Digitaria* references the finger-like look of all the species in this genus. There are two introduced species that are considered pests: smooth crabgrass (*D. ischaemum*) and hairy crabgrass (*D. sanguinalis*). Both opportunistically take advantage of bare patches in lawns where the grass is struggling.

Crabgrass is the easier of the two weeds to control, as it is an annual, warm-season grass with fibrous roots. It can be removed wherever it is found by simply digging it out. Mow your grass regularly to ensure that it doesn't have a chance to develop seed heads, and if perchance it does flower and set seeds, make sure to put the clippings in the garbage, rather than composting them.

Quackgrass (*Elytrigia repens*), on the other hand, is a serious invasive weed. It goes by many common names besides quackgrass: couch grass, twitch grass, quick grass, and devil's weed. Native to Europe and Western Asia, it arrived in North America as a weed in cereal crops. It is a temperate or cool-season perennial grass. Quackgrass is hardy through all plant zones, establishes quickly, and spreads through rhizomatous roots, as well as by seed that is blown on the wind to new areas. Control is difficult as any small piece of root with a node left in the soil will become a new plant in short order. While it is tempting to resort to chemicals to control this devilish weed, we prefer manual control where we are literally on our hands and knees removing the long roots by hand. Once an area is cleared, do not presume that it is gone, but rather go back and check for any new green growth and get those immature plants out right away. Like many gardeners, we have considerable experience in dealing with quackgrass. In my garden, this is the only technique that works for the long run. That, and eternal vigilance. But we much prefer dealing with quackgrass than with creeping bellflower!

Quackgrass is a cool-season perennial grass. Unlike crabgrass, which generally grows low to the ground, quackgrass can quickly become tall if left unchecked.

The best control for both weeds is to have a healthy lawn with deep roots to combat drought stress. Spreading a fine compost over the lawn in spring and fall will serve to build up organic matter in the underlying soil that will hold moisture in the soil longer. Compost will build up soil fertility so that the lawn species will be able to access needed nutrients beyond the high-nitrogen fertilizers usually applied. To deter either quackgrass or crabgrass in garden beds, use mulch, either living or organic, which will deter seeds from landing and germinating quickly. Both your garden and lawn will thank you by being healthier and hopefully will be more weed-free![7] —JM

Thistles: They are everywhere!
What can I do to control them?

Thistles are a common denizen of gardens, waste areas, ditches, construction sites, agricultural fields, rangelands, woodlands, riparian areas . . . pretty much anywhere there is soil. They are ridiculously prolific and spread via seed as well as through a significant root system. Thistles are not native to North America—they were introduced from Europe (yes, even the so-called Canada thistle!). They can be a huge issue in agricultural crops and in gardens, where they muscle out cultivated plants.

Thistles are biennial; they produce leaves in the first year and flowers in the second. If you see a flowering thistle, you'll know that is has already had at least one year to get its root system established.

There are four main thistle species you'll likely come across on the prairies:

*   Canada thistle (*Cirsium arvense*) is commonly found in grasslands (and in your garden!). Canada thistle reaches a height of up to 4 feet (1.2 metres), with lobed, lance-shaped leaves tipped with spines. The purple or pink flowers measure up to 3/4 inches (2 centimetres) in diameter. Once they are spent, the flowers are transformed into dandelion-like seeds with white wings (pappi) to facilitate wind dispersal. Each plant can have up to 1,500 seeds. Canada thistles have long fleshy taproots, which makes them difficult to dig up. ·

*   Nodding thistle, also known as musk thistle (*Carduus nutans*), is another grassland plant. Nodding thistle has large, nodding purple flowers (other thistles have upright flowers). Thorny bracts sit just below the flower heads. The leaves are lobed and spiny, with an easily identifiable white midrib. The stems are pointy and hairy, and grow up to eight inches (twenty centimetres) tall.

*   Marsh thistle (*Cirsium palustre*) and plumeless thistle (*Carduus acanthoides*) prefer wet, riparian environments. Plumeless thistle has small single flower heads borne on each

*Canada thistle is one of the
most common species of thistle
you may find in your garden.*

branch. The basal leaves are large, and the size of the leaves decreases near the top of the stem. Marsh thistle bears flowers in clusters on the tips of each stem. The flowers do not have spiny bracts. Unlike other thistles, the stems do not branch until the very top of the plant; as well, marsh thistle has fibrous roots instead of a taproot. The leaves are hairy and lobed, up to eight inches (twenty centimetres) long at the base.

Thistles are best removed by digging before the flowers set seed. Bear in mind that any root pieces left over are likely to create new plants. Tackling thistles when they are in their first year of growth may be more effective than waiting until they are more established. Persistent mowing will remove flower heads and gradually—*very* gradually—cause the plants to weaken.

If you feel that no other option is available, there are herbicides formulated to work on thistles. Remember that removing only the above-ground parts does not work. Follow the package directions cautiously and to the letter, and be sure to wear all necessary protective clothing during application.[8]—SN

Using vinegar in the garden for pest control or as a herbicide— yay or nay?

White vinegar, containing 5 percent acetic acid, and pickling vinegar, with 7 percent acetic acid, are often touted as weed killers, and, indeed, there are many acetic acid products registered for use as herbicides in Canada.[9] Unfortunately, vinegar has such a low concentration of acetic acid that although it may be able to kill leafy plant parts, it doesn't usually slam the root systems. These vinegars are best saved for salad dressing and preserving vegetables.

You can source stronger products containing 10 percent, 12 percent or 20 percent acetic acid, and with repeated applications, they may work much better on weeds and unwanted turfgrass, but may damage other plants' root systems.

Our recommendation is to pull weeds and dig up undesirable turfgrass whenever possible. This can be a tedious and time-consuming task and is ongoing for the life of the garden, but it is the safest option.

Regarding pesticides, there are none containing acetic acid registered with Health Canada for use as a control for ants or other insects.[10] Pouring vinegar over anthills to break up ant activity is a common gardening tactic, however.

Remember that the superstrength acetic acid products can cause serious burns and permanent injuries if proper equipment is not worn and safety protocols are not implemented.—**SN**

The Creepy
and the Crawly:
Insect Pests

2

Aphids: They are attacking in hordes! What can I do?

Black aphids are sucking the juices out of the stems of these chervil plants.

Aphids are not one of those insects that you can eliminate once and for all or even truly prevent an infestation of. They are pretty much a gardening mainstay—a problem that many gardeners face year after year. These sap eaters will attack nearly anything that has leaves and stems (although some species favour certain plants). The feeding damage can be harmful enough, but it can also lead to the introduction of certain types of fungi. Even more seriously, aphids can also be vectors for some plant viruses.

Aphids can reproduce both sexually and asexually. The whole idea that female aphids hatch from overwintered eggs in a pregnant state is absolutely true, and one female can produce numerous generations over the summer. When you consider the fact that it takes a mere week for nymphs to mature and give birth to thousands of aphids, you can see how they definitely have numbers on their side. Fortunately, if you follow the tenets of Integrated Pest Management and watch for them to make an appearance, you will be able to act quickly and keep your plants from sustaining too much damage. Look for plant stems that are turning yellow, or foliage that is suddenly wilting or curling. Bear in mind that these symptoms can indicate other problems instead—the best way to tell if you have an aphid problem is to spot the insects themselves. The adults have a distinctive pear-shaped body and can be grey, black, or green in colour. Some species even sport what looks like fine hairs on their bodies.

The simplest way to deal with aphids is to blast them off the plants with water from your garden hose (use the strongest jet you have on your nozzle attachment). You can also use a soft damp cloth or even an old pair of gardening gloves to wipe them from plants and subsequently crush them. You will probably have to repeat these tasks a few times until you see favourable results, but at least the effort required is minimal. If you have a greenhouse, releasing ladybug beetles may be useful as each beetle will chow down on a huge quantity of aphids. You can also release ladybugs out into the open, but they may not stay completely focused on the aphids in your yard, as it's a big, wide world out there (although, if you have a lot of the pests, the beetles will usually stick around until they've finished them off).

Remember that adult aphids will lay their eggs on plants in the fall, hoping to successfully overwinter. Thwart that plan by spraying perennial plants with water and cleaning up the debris from annual plants.[1]—SN

Ants have taken over the wooden post of a raised garden bed.

Ants: They are invading everything!

Ants are highly social, co-operative insects that act for the good of the colony. Within a garden, they act as scavengers, soil aerators, pest suppressors, and seed transporters.

Yet in our gardens and sometimes in our homes they can become pests if their numbers become out of balance within those environments. Our job as gardeners is to ensure that the environments we create in our gardens are in balance.

Trying to remove ants by killing them will only work temporarily as their numbers dwarf humans. They will simply move back in again unless the environment changes. The best way to address the problem is to improve the soil within our gardens by adding organic matter on an annual basis, so that it has the capacity to hold moisture. Ants love to take up homes in dry fine soils and avoid moist complex soils. This includes lawns where the soil underneath is often depleted.

Add lots of compost and manure to boost that organic matter in your garden, then ensure that the soils stay evenly moist throughout the season, which co-incidentally is just what our plants need too. Lawns benefit from an annual or semi-annual application of compost that is raked down into the roots, which will over time improve the soil structure below.

Short-term remedies to move or disperse ants can include adding wet, sloppy, smelly coffee grounds to where their colony is located or using cinnamon, cloves, baby powder, or citrus purée across their trails or around sensitive plants. Or spray vinegar over the colony.

Planting mint beside doorways and in garden beds is an old-fashioned but tried-and-true method to deter ants from coming inside, as the smell repels ants. Making a spray from steeped mint with a few drops of dishwashing soap and spraying areas where you want to dine or relax can also be effective in the short term.

In the end, though, we as gardeners need to realize that just as picnics can't happen without ants, gardens need ants to be healthy too. —JM

Talk to me about the whole peony and ant thing. What is the truth of this relationship?

Peonies have waxy bud scales that curl tightly over the bud. The scales contain nectar, a tantalizing food source, which attracts ants by the hundreds. Many gardeners believe that without the presence of ants on the buds, the scales will remain closed, and the flowers will not be able to unfurl.

In reality, ants and peonies are a terrific example of "mutualism," where both species benefit from an intricate symbiotic relationship. Just like plants have developed flowers with nectar and fragrance to attract pollinators, other insect-plant relationships have evolved to attract insects to protect plants from herbivores and other predators.

Ants are good protectors of their source of nectar and will crowd and run off other insects that try to steal a sip. The peony flowers are not damaged by the ants, and, in this way, other insects that may feed on the flowers (and possibly other plant parts) are prohibited from doing so. By expending a significant amount of energy to produce nectar to attract ants, peonies, in effect, are saving themselves from predators. It's a win-win for everyone involved![2] —JM & SN

Ants and peonies have a mutualistic relationship. Here, a ladybug has joined in on the fun!

When we talk about "pesticides," what do we mean?

Pesticides are any chemicals used to control organisms that harm plants. Pesticides is an umbrella term that includes substances used to kill insects (insecticides), weeds or unwanted plant material (herbicides), fungi (fungicides), molluscs such as slugs (molluscacides), rodents (rodenticides), mites (acaricides), and others.

Cutworms: How do I ID them and keep them from eating my plants?

What we label "cutworms" are the larvae of several different species of moths. They are caterpillars, not worms. They can be green, grey, or black in colour, with a variety of stripes and spots (or none at all). They usually grow up to two inches (five centimetres) in length.

Cutworms can be extremely efficient plant killers. They usually attack at night and can decimate entire rows of seedlings in mere hours. Cutworms are most active in early spring, and seem to go after tender young plants over mature ones. They don't appear to have a preference for certain types of vegetables and flowers—they'll munch on everything. Cutworms cleanly chew through the stems of plants at the base of the soil, and they will also eat plant roots, cutting off the plants just beneath the soil. If you go out in the morning and see all of your plants bitten off tidily at ground level, it's likely the work of cutworms and not the dainty nibbling of deer or rabbits, who usually gnaw off upper growth.

If you want to manually remove cutworms, go out at dusk, at night (take a flash-light), or in the very early morning. Cutworms will curl up into a little ring when they're not moving, which makes them a bit easier to spot. Look for them at the base of plant stems, at the soil level. Pick them with gloved hands, throw them into a bucket of soapy water, and discard.

Keep the area around your veggie plants absolutely weed-free. This helps control the spread of cutworms because they like laying their eggs on plants that are not their food sources, such as grass. Cutworm eggs hatch in the fall and produce larvae that burrow into the soil to overwinter, readying themselves to feed in the spring. If you eliminate the places they can lay eggs, there will be less of a problem. A favourite method for dealing with cutworms involves creating collars and plopping them overtop of young plants as soon as the seeds germinate. Raid your recycling bin, and use empty toilet paper rolls or empty and clean single-serve yogourt cups with the bottoms cut out. Sink the collars about two inches (five centimetres) into the soil. Leave them in place until the plants get big enough to almost fill them—by that time, the cutworms should have lost interest and moved on. If you use yogourt cups, you can clean them and save them for the next spring.

If you wish to exercise the option, you can try a biological control called BTK (*Bacillus thuringiensis*), but bear in mind that it will kill any caterpillar in the area, even the good ones. Another option is to sprinkle diatomaceous earth on the soil at the base of the affected plants. Cutworms do not like the sharp grit of the diatoms. But if it rains or you irrigate, you will have to reapply the diatomaceous earth. And remember that diatomaceous earth doesn't discriminate — you might take down good bugs with the bad. We recommend using cultural and physical controls instead.[3] — SN

How do I deal with red lily beetles?

The dreaded red or scarlet lily beetle (*Lilioceris lilii*), which can infest lilies, is a non-native invasive species from Asia that arrived in Canada and the northeastern United States fifty years ago. It made its way to Alberta in 2004, appearing in Edmonton in 2017, as a frantic call from an Edmonton friend informed me.

This is one smart insect as it has multiple defences against predators, ranging from fire-red colouring that shrieks danger to would-be diners, to the ability to fall off a plant and land upside down so its black underside blends in with soil. In addition, the larvae cover themselves with their own excrement, which makes them less appealing to predators, and they lay tiny eggs on the undersides of leaves out of sight. In Asia there are parasitic wasps that keep them in check by laying their eggs in the red lily beetles' larvae. Dr. Ken Fry from Olds College in Olds, Alberta, together with researchers from Carleton University in Ottawa, has been conducting trial releases of one of these parasitic wasps, *Tetrastichus setifer*, at Olds College and in other locations in Alberta. The key to success is whether these wasps can survive our winters.

Until then, manual control is really the only answer. In early spring, watch for the adults to emerge from the soil where they overwinter. Pick them off and drop them into a bucket of soapy water (make sure it has a lid in case they try to escape). Try planting checkered lily (*Fritillaria meleagris*) in the fall, as they are early spring bloomers and will attract the emerging adult beetles to them, which you can then quickly remove. But do not relax. Regularly inspect your lilies for the tiny eggs or really gross-looking larvae feasting on the undersides.

Enlist your neighbours in the battle because if these beetles are in your garden, they will soon be in theirs, and vigilance must be eternal if you want any of the lily species to thrive.[4] — JM

Red lily beetles are deadly in both adult and larval forms.

There are fungus gnats in my containers. What can I do to combat them?

Occasionally, when you buy houseplants or bring plants in from the outdoors in the autumn with the intent to overwinter them, you may all of a sudden notice what seems like hundreds of tiny (1/8-to-1/6-inch or 3-to-4-millimetre) flying insects. These little guys are fungus gnats. There are several different species, all of them from the order Diptera.

Although extremely annoying, fungus gnats are not harmful to plants while in their flying adult stage. (They are also not capable of biting humans or animals.) They love damp soil, especially if it has not been freshly changed. They cannot fly very well, so they usually stick close to the soil and become more active when you water or move the containers around.

Fungus gnats have a life cycle of approximately one month. Adult females will lay 150 to 200 eggs in the soil, then die. The eggs hatch in a week and the larvae feed for about fourteen days before pupating. The adults emerge one week later, to drive everyone crazy for about ten days. The larval stage is the most harmful to plants, as the insects feed on plant roots and can potentially (although rarely) spread plant pathogens that can cause diseases such as root rot, collar rot, and damping off.

Fortunately, it is fairly easy to eliminate fungus gnats, although it takes persistence and patience. First, ensure the soil is not too damp. Water only when necessary, and remove all standing water. Make sure your containers have proper drainage and that the soil is sufficiently aerated. If the infestation is severe, you can carefully scrape off the top layer of soil and replenish it with new soil. (Repotting entirely is another option if you are faced with a huge infestation.) You can get little yellow sticky traps in garden centres and some big-box stores; these are excellent, non-toxic solutions, although you may have to frequently change the brightly coloured tape.[5]—SN

My delphiniums are being ravaged by small worms. What can I do to stop this from happening?

Delphiniums are one of our favourite old-fashioned perennials, along with monkshood and larkspur. As gardeners, we are also constantly frustrated that they are a favourite feast for the caterpillar delphinium leaftier. It does us no good to complain as they are a native species that historically was drawn to our native tall larkspur (*Delphinium glaucum*) and Nuttall's larkspur (*Delphinium nuttallianum*). They find our local garden varieties really tasty as well.

The first sign of a problem is when you discover the tops of new shoots on your delphinium plant are stuck together and a small worm is feasting inside. The only control is to pick them off and dispose of them, but the damage is often done in terms of reduced flowering, though the plants themselves are not seriously affected.

You now know that your garden is home to this rather beautiful golden moth, who will lay her eggs at the base of your delphiniums at the end of summer. Once hatched, young larvae will overwinter next to the plants in soil and in the plant litter on the ground, even inside the dried hollow stems. In the spring, the caterpillars will climb up the new shoots until they reach the tops, and hide inside, away from predators, where the good stuff is found.

The best course of action is good garden hygiene and manual control. In the fall, cut back the stems of your plants right to soil level. This will disrupt overwintering habitat. Then, in spring, once the plants are up and about twelve inches (thirty centimetres) tall, remove the top six inches (fifteen centimetres) of all shoots, as the caterpillars will have already emerged and be up on top. Dispose of the shoots in the garbage, not in your compost. The plants will send up new flowering shoots, but be vigilant in case the timing was off.

The good news is that there is only one generation per year, but do not relax and assume that you are in the clear after one season. Make a habit of cutting back old stalks and new stems in the fall and spring, and you will once again enjoy your delphinium and monkshood plants. —JM

Tiny beetles are munching holes in my *Brassica* plants (cabbages, broccoli, cauliflower, etc.) and in some of my leafy greens. How can I stop them from doing this?

If you have *Brassica* plants that look like tiny buckshot has been aimed at them, then you have flea beetles. Members of the leaf beetle family Chrysomelidae, flea beetles are not just one species but many, with three species in particular infesting *Brassica* crops on the prairies. The hop flea beetle (*Psylliodes punctulata*) is a native species, but the crucifer flea beetle (*Phyllotreta cruciferae*) and the striped flea beetle (*P. striolata*) are both introduced species. There are other flea beetles that infest other edibles (such as potatoes) and ornamental species.

Understanding the life cycle of flea beetles is critical to managing their presence in the garden. There is only one generation per season, with overwintering adults emerging after the first warm period in April or May. Different species will appear earlier or later, but the average amount of time is ten days after the leaf litter thaws. The beetles will feast on seedlings and lay eggs at the base of *Brassica* plants during the month of May. After the eggs hatch, the beetles will then emerge as adults later in the summer to once again feed before overwintering. The larvae also do damage to germinating seeds, taproots, and root hairs, causing tunnelling in root brassicas and stunting growth in other crops.

Flea beetles are always present during warm and dry springs. These conditions are favourable to an explosion of beetle populations, which can do noticeable damage. Cooler and wetter springs will cut populations somewhat, but flea beetles are a highly resilient species, so do not count on such springs to be a cure-all.

To avoid the worst of the damage to your plants, consider waiting to seed or transplant seedlings until after the adult insects have emerged and flown on after not finding anything in your garden to munch. Alternatively, sow radishes and mustard greens throughout the season as a trap or sacrificial crop. Interplanting species of the mint family, Lamiaceae, such as basil, catmint, and thyme, is effective as the scent of these plants repels the beetles, or at least confuses them. Using a physical barrier such as a floating row cover after sowing or planting will be effective against visiting adults looking to lay eggs. To be a strong barrier, the row cover must be firmly anchored with no gaps for adult beetles to get in. Another barrier to deter emerging adults is diatomaceous earth, but be careful with its use in alkaline soils, as it is composed of fossilized skeletons of diatoms, which contain silica. The sharp edges of the silica are likened to broken glass that damages the "skins" of the beetles. A homemade alcohol and soap spray may be effective, or at least make you feel better! The recipe is two parts rubbing alcohol to five parts water, plus a tablespoon (fifteen millilitres) of mild bio-degradable soap (not detergent). Please test any spray on a few plants first before using wholesale to ensure that your mixture will not cause burning of leaves.

If you are experiencing severe infestations, crop rotation is always a course of action, and will require that you not plant any *Brassica* species in your garden bed for two or three seasons. This action will eliminate overwintering populations. When you resume planting *Brassica* edibles, make sure to use physical barriers to avoid setting up another cycle of infestation.

Always remember too that while the leaves of your plants may look like they have been used as target practice, they are still doing their job of photosynthesizing and are perfectly edible.[6] —JM

Flea beetle damage is easy to spot—
the leaves of your plants will be
covered in tiny holes.

I'm noticing white moths all over my cabbages and other plants in the same family. What are they?

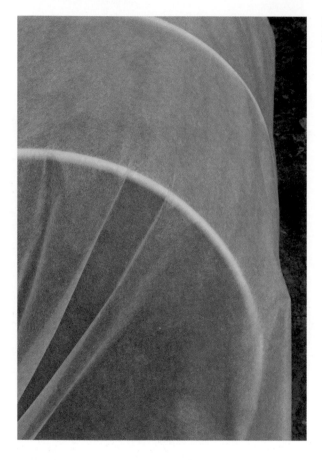

Use floating row cover fabric to deter cabbage moths.

Those lovely moths fluttering over your cabbages and other members of the Brassicaceae family are cabbage moths (*Mamestra brassicae*), or possibly an introduced species called the cabbage white butterfly (*Pieris rapae*). They are looking for a safe place to lay their tiny white or orange eggs on the undersides of leaves of their preferred host plants and are really motivated to procreate!

The problem with cabbage moths arises when the eggs hatch and the larvae become small green "worms" that feast on the foliage of your edibles. They can make Swiss cheese out of your cabbage and strip kale leaves to the nub before they reach adulthood. In addition, some species of Solanaceae, such as tomatoes, and, on occasion, sunflowers are also host plants.

To prevent your cabbages and other edibles in this family from becoming nurseries, use a physical barrier to completely cover the plants from the time you sow seeds or plant seedlings until after harvesting. Floating row cover fabric, made from spun polyester, is perfect for the job as it lets in air and moisture, so it can remain over the plants all season long. The fabric can be used over hoops or loosely placed right over the garden bed, but there cannot be any gaps to let the moths in. I generally mound up soil over the edges of the fabric, along where it meets the soil, or use bricks to anchor the cloth in windy locations, and I make sure that the openings at either end of the bed are always well secured. Even then, I monitor constantly for visitors.

Some gardeners use other plants as decoys to keep the moths away. Species of the mint family, Lamiaceae, or the onion genus, *Allium*, with their strong scents, can either decoy or repel the moths. Sage, lavender, and chives planted beside *Brassica* edibles can also serve this purpose well. Sowing crimson clover or peas and interplanting *Brassica* seedlings can be effective strategies, too. One year I had a cover crop of field peas growing with the idea that I would repeatedly "chop and drop" the foliage as green mulch, then I would interplant cabbage seedlings. Well, the peas got away from me, and I was too tender-hearted to chop them back once they started flowering, so the cabbage grew amid the dense surrounding of peas all summer. Not a single cabbage moth found those cabbages that year!

Scouting for eggs and removing them from the leaves with a swipe of your gloved hand is also effective, as the action will remove that year's generation from your plants. But be vigilant as there can be two or even three generations per year.

Good luck! —JM

What is that white foam on the stems of my plants? What can I do about it?

Inside that foam is a spittlebug or froghopper, the nymph of the Cercopidae family. There are some 23,000 species within the family, but, despite the numbers, they really pose little harm to the garden.

Spittlebugs lay their eggs in late summer, and they overwinter among the plant and leaf litter. In spring the eggs hatch and green nymphs climb up the plants. Once they find a handy spot, usually in the leaf axils, they secret the foam that alerts us to their presence. The foam serves to keep the immature insects hydrated and cool, plus it provides shelter and safety from predators.

If you are curious about who resides inside, gently remove the foam, and inside you will see a rather cute, tiny green insect. In the summer, we often see the tan, frog-like adults hopping in the garden, and don't really think much about them as they go about their business.

While inside the foam, the nymphs will feed on plant sap. You may see some damage to plant stems as a result, but the damage is usually minimal, and plants can easily overcome any deformities caused by the feeding. It's not worth getting "het up" about their presence unless the spittlebug is attached to a favourite plant or the damage is reducing productivity, say, in strawberries. A good spray from the garden hose will usually do the job of removing them.

If populations do get out of hand, the best control is a good cleanup of plant matter in the fall, so they are not able to overwinter.[7] —JM

The foam that harbours
spittlebugs isn't pretty, but the
insects themselves aren't seriously
harmful to your plants.

What is the best way of dealing with wasp nests?

An unwelcome sight in the garden: the nest of a paper wasp.

The natural inclination of most people once they find a wasp's nest in their garden is to get rid of it. As predators ourselves, we have the instinct to deal rather permanently with something that is a real or perceived threat. Wasps as predators have the same instinct and are just as cranky as human beings. However, they only have limited defences such as stinging and biting. We have more defences, including chemicals that can kill them on the spot.

Before going after the nest, though, do consider that wasps are beneficial insects. And they are necessary in the grand scheme of things. They belong to the same order as bees and ants and are important pollinators. As predators, they also hunt insects that are considered pests, such as caterpillars, weevils, and maggots.

Secondly, make sure that the insects are wasps. Many bees mimic wasps in appearance and are ground nesters, as are yellow-jacket wasps (*Vespula* spp.), the ones we most often associate with wasps. Paper wasps are vespid wasps, and are responsible for the papery wasp nests hanging from eaves, trees, and other inconvenient spots in the garden. There are also a myriad of parasitoid wasps that don't even look like what we believe a wasp should look like. They lay their eggs in other insects, often ones we consider pests, and as the eggs hatch, they then kill the insects.

Most of the time, when I have wasp nests in the gardens, I ignore them. Like humans, if you don't get in their faces, they will leave you alone.

However, should a nest be in a location where you will get in the wasps' way, or if someone in your house, visitors, or neighbours are allergic to their venom, it is wise to deal with it. Wait until the cool of the evening or early morning when they are not as active, and simply blast the nest apart with a jet of water, then quickly go inside! Once the nest is gone, the wasps will linger for a bit, but then disperse as they will need to find another location. If the nest is in the ground, be aware that the entrance may be a tunnel and the main nest could be some distance away. I once had a nest in my compost, and I turned the hose at full force into the entrance and then, thinking I had destroyed it, stuck my fork into the compost to turn it, only to find the nest intact and a mass of rather upset wasps. Needless to say, I set a new land record for speed exiting the garden!

If you choose to use wasp-killer chemicals, be aware that the chemicals are dangerous to humans (especially children) and the environment. Only use as much as necessary rather than emptying the can. We often go overboard spraying, and if the chemicals are broad spectrum, they will kill other insects. You also must clean up all the dead wasps and debris as they are also poisonous to pets and other mammals. Calling professionals to eliminate a wasp nest with pesticides is the preferred course of action. There are also sprays that are not highly toxic that use ingredients such as peppermint oils instead of chemicals.

Deterring wasps from nesting in your garden is the better option, so do make sure that unwanted food, including bird and pet food, is not left out. Garbage cans or bins should be closed tightly. Inspect your house, sheds, and other structures for cracks, crevices, and other holes that make ideal locations to start building a nest. Wasp decoy nests, be they paper bags or crafted ones, can be helpful as wasps will tend to avoid creating a nest close by. Using essential oils, such as peppermint, lemongrass, clove, and scented geranium, soaked into pads and hung up or placed where wasps might decide to build a nest can also be a good deterrent. Plants with strong aromas will also deter wasps, with wormwood (*Artemisia* spp.) species and members of the mint family (Lamiaceae) being particularly effective.

In the end, what we really need to do is educate ourselves about wasps, their behaviours, and their important role in our gardens.[8] —JM

How can I attract native bees to my yard? Do those store-bought houses work?

Native or wild bees are in serious decline across western Canada. Degradation or loss of habitat is one of the main reasons for the decline. Widespread use of pesticides and competition from non-native bees and non-native plants are further stressors.

Absolutely, our native bees prefer the diversity of the wild areas, be they established parks, where habitat is preserved, or rural areas, where habitat is left for them to thrive. However, urban areas are an increasingly important habitat for our native bees, primarily because of the potential biodiversity that many of our gardens and parks all offer, providing different niches for our bees.

Native bees are not just the favourite bumblebees. There are also leafcutter and mason bees. Other species include plasterer bees, sweat bees (also known as halictid bees), digger bees, and andrenid bees. Some look more like wasps—from which they evolved—or are easily mistaken as flies. Honeybees are not native to Canada. They originated in Europe and have been managed and regulated as agricultural livestock.

Native bees love sunny, well-lit gardens, with lots of biodiversity of plants. Native plants are their choice as bees have co-evolved with these plants over aeons.

Bees have good colour vision and especially like blue, purple, violet, white, and yellow flowers. Each species has different tongue lengths, which have been adapted to different flowers, so a variety of flower shapes will benefit a diversity of bees. Bumblebees are divided into long-tongued and short-tongued species. Leafcutter bees, with their short tongues and large bodies, cannot access long tubular flowers like penstemon and will stick to visiting upright flowers with short clustered florets, like native sunflowers.

Examples of diversity of plants for bees include: bee balm (*Monarda* spp.), black-eyed Susan (*Rudbeckia hirta*), stonecrop (*Hylotelephium* spp.), goldenrod (*Solidago* spp.), purple coneflower (*Echinacea purpurea*), Joe Pye weed (*Eupatorium purpureum*), prairie crocus (*Anemone patens*), sunflower (*Helianthus annuus and H. maximiliani*), geranium (*Geranium* spp.), prairie sage or white sage (*Artemisia ludoviciana*), and blanket flower (*Gaillardia aristata*). Many other common garden perennials and annuals will attract generalist bees, but it is important that those chosen are not hybridized as those are often cultivars that have reduced nectar or pollen. Do plant flowers in masses, so that the bees can see them, and plant a continuous range of flowers over the season, especially in early spring and late fall when many a garden is lacking those important nectar and pollen sources.

Do provide multiple areas for nesting. Many native bees are ground nesters and need access to bare earth to burrow inside to make their nests. Mulching garden beds is important for many reasons, but leaving some bare areas for the bees is also crucial. Provide old logs or stumps, but not ones where you have drilled holes. Bees that excavate holes in wood will do so themselves, and it is possible to go overboard in creating nesting, which encourages a surge in bee populations that cannot be supported by available flora. In an out-of-the-way spot, leave branches, sticks, and other bracken, which other species will take advantage of as viable nesting. Consider sowing clover in the lawn, where it will flower and provide forage in an area that is usually a "desert" for bees. Provide leafcutter and mason bees with old dried stalks that are hollow, or simply leave some of your perennial stalks up when you cut them back after flowering.

Bees also need landing spots for resting, foraging, and drinking water. Providing a shallow dish with mud and small stones will allow them to pause and drink. Even a patch of soil kept moist will serve this purpose.

Lastly, creating microclimates that provide shelter from the weather will help wild bees thrive in the garden.

It seems obvious, but do not use synthetic pesticides and use organic pesticides minimally. Working to create a healthy diverse garden with great soil will ensure that the need for this sort of pest control is minimized. If you use a pesticide, make sure that you apply it when there are no bees and other pollinators active.

Additionally, we recommend not having a backyard hive of honeybees, unless you are doing so to harvest honey. The numbers of honeybees in a hive will outcompete the native bees for resources.

Creating houses for bumblebees, leafcutter, and mason bees is something that concerned people are doing in droves these days. They can be effective in attracting bees if there are no other nesting spots made in the garden. They are also important if you are a citizen scientist participating in the Bumble Bee Watch project (bumblebeewatch.org) or other research that assists conservationists with data collection.

Maintaining bee houses requires that you clean and sanitize them each year after the bees have departed. There are many pests affecting bees, and good hygiene is essential, as an uncleaned house that is reused can spread pathogens and encourage insect pests.

Bumblebee houses are simply constructed with a lid that can be opened to remove the raw cotton that is used as nesting material. Sanitize with 10 percent bleach, and set it out again. A good plan for constructing your own bumblebee house can be found on the Alberta Native Bee Council website (alberta nativebeecouncil.ca).

Leafcutter and mason bee houses should be easy to open. Carefully remove cocoons if they are overwintering in your refrigerator. You will then be able to clean the nesting trays. The length of the tubes should be between six and eight inches (fifteen to twenty centimetres) as the bees lay female eggs in the back and male eggs in the front. If the tubes are too short, there will be only male eggs. Waffle board or nesting trays are better than the bamboo stems often found in commercially made houses. Do have a front panel on your house to deter parasitoids, woodpeckers, and other predators from disturbing the cocoons. Materials for the bees to line and plug their nests will need to be close by. Mason bees like dense clay, and leafcutter bees prefer flat, easily rolled leaves.

Consider the size of your garden before deciding how many houses to install. The average garden can support one or two houses.

Do not be discouraged if bees do not find the nest for a couple of seasons. Keep the house clean and ready and eventually a bee will find it to be a new home.[9]—JM

Prairie crocus (Anemone patens) is a beautiful and useful bee plant.

What can I do about the leafhoppers on my Virginia creeper, Engelmann ivy, or grapevines?

While leafhoppers are not particular about the types of plants they consume—most flowering perennials and annuals are fair game, as are roses—they absolutely love vines such as grapes, Virginia creeper, and Engelmann ivy. If you're out weeding in the garden on a hot dry midsummer day, you'll likely disturb clouds of the jumping critters. Leafhoppers are slender, small (1/4 inch or 6 millimetres long) white or yellow insects with sap-sucking mouthparts. Both the adults and the nymphs attach themselves to the undersides of leaves. As they feed, the top sides of the leaves become stippled with white specks. Prolonged feeding will cause the leaves to turn yellow and dry up. Healthy vines can usually deal with the leaf drop that occurs as a result of leafhopper trouble. The problem with repeated infestations over several years, however, is that the plants eventually weaken and may be harmed by other plants and diseases.

Leafhopper eggs hatch in early spring, and it takes about three weeks before the wingless nymphs become adults. The adults lay a fresh batch of eggs in the autumn, but you probably won't notice them, as the eggs do not sit on the outside of stems and leaves, but are rather inserted in small openings that the insects create in plant tissues.[10]

Some leafhoppers are vectors for aster yellows, a relatively uncommon disease in home gardens. (It occurs more frequently in commercial agriculture, particularly in plants such as canola.) Leafhoppers that have fed on infected plants transmit the pathogen to healthy plants. In its bid to survive, thrive, and reproduce, the infected host plant can do some pretty strange things. The plant may stop growing or grow very tall, very quickly. What should normally be floral plant parts may develop as leafy parts (all the more appealing to leafhoppers!), or the plant can take on a green colour that it is not supposed to have. The tubers of vegetable plants may grow an unusually large number of root hairs or become disfigured and discoloured. Aster yellows can overwinter in the roots of perennial plants. The pathogen spreads only via the infected insects—it is not dispersed by wind or splashed up into plants with rainwater or irrigation, nor does it sit in the soil. Eradicating aster yellows in the garden can be accomplished only by controlling leafhopper populations and removing infected plants, so that the cycle is interrupted.[11]

To control leafhoppers, try the following methods:

1. Sticky yellow tape traps placed near the vines will catch some of the adult insects while they're bouncing around, but you will need a lot of traps to make a dent in the population.
2. Strong blasts of water from the garden hose may also work to dislodge them from plants, but repeated applications will definitely be required, and you'll likely want to use this method in conjunction with other controls.
3. Be sure to keep up with the weeding in your garden. If the weeds have the upper hand in your garden, leafhoppers may find them first. If your prized plants are growing nearby, the insects are likely to cruise over and sample them.
4. Leafhoppers have plenty of enemies besides gardeners: They are food for insects such as ladybugs, spiders, and damselflies. Allow these beneficial insects (and arachnids) to do their work, and don't discourage them by using pesticides.
5. If you feel you have no other choice, persistent, frequent applications of commercially manufactured insecticidal soaps may work. (Remember, it is not advised to use a detergent-based recipe you've mixed yourself.) Timing is everything, however! It is best to treat leafhoppers while they are in the nymph stage and not in their more active adult stage, so if you can catch them early in their life cycle, you'll have more success. Because hitting that brief window of opportunity is extremely difficult, you may have to tackle the adults as well by using insecticidal soap every five to seven days. Leafhoppers do not move as much in the very early morning and late in the evening, so try the chemical then. Make sure you coat both the top and undersides of the leaves. Bear in mind that insecticidal soap is not the least toxic option to use, and it can harm any insects that are exposed to it. If you decide to use it, be sure to follow all label instructions exactly and wear protective equipment and clothing. Do not allow children or pets into the area after applying.[12] —SN

There are small round growths on the leaves and branches of my burr oak tree. Some of them are fuzzy, but I've seen hard ones as well. I've also noticed a weird mossy-like ball on my rose bush. What causes these oddities and what should I do about them?

There are hundreds of species of gall wasps in the Cynipidae family, but the evidence of a couple of them is commonly found on burr oak trees in prairie gardens. The woolly oak gall wasp (*Andricus ignotus*) will produce fuzzy, grey, round or oval growths primarily found on oak tree leaves, while the bullet gall wasp (*Disholcaspis* spp.) creates hard oval galls, bullet-like in appearance and woody in texture, in the tree branches. The galls are green when first formed and turn to brown when dried. They are an abnormal growth that forms when the eggs are laid and as the tree responds to the feeding activity of the larvae. They serve as both protection and a source of food for the larvae. (The adult wasps do not eat.)

The great thing about these galls is that although they are weird-looking and may stick around on a tree for years, they won't do any harm to the tree. Adult wasps are less than 1/4 inch (6 millimetres) long and are likely not even on your radar. Bullet and woolly oak gall wasps produce two generations annually.[13]

Another type of cynipid wasp creates galls on the leaves, stems, buds, or even the roots of roses. The mossy rose gall wasp (*Diplolepis rosae*) is responsible for strangely beautiful bright red balls of fuzzy filaments that resemble moss.

Mossy rose gall wasps produce only one generation per year. Adults lay their eggs in the spring. The larvae feed during the summer and overwinter in the gall that has been created on the rose plant. The next generation of adults emerges in the spring, ready to begin a new cycle.[14]

If you see galls on your burr oak trees or your roses, you don't have to do anything to remove them—just allow nature to take its course. (Dried bullet galls will often fall off the tree of their own accord over the winter.) If there are a massive number of galls on one branch, development of that particular limb may be

Mossy rose galls have weird, flowerlike structures.

slowed, so in rare cases, you may wish to remove woolly or bullet galls left on a tree by hand. (Be extremely careful not to scrape off any bark in the process.) Mossy galls on roses may be cut out using a pair of secateurs (pruning shears). Try to remove the galls while they are still fresh and green, in late spring or early summer, before the adult wasps have emerged. If the galls are brown and are punctured by tiny holes, the wasps have already left. The dried galls do not take any nutrients from trees.[15]

Insecticidal soaps and other chemicals cannot penetrate the galls and harm the insects inside.

Woodpeckers and other birds prey on gall wasps, so creating a bird-friendly environment may be helpful in preventing gall formation. Provide a secure haven for birds to live, gather food, and nest in. Offer a diverse range of plants that have fruit, seeds, and nuts. A combination of coniferous and deciduous trees and low hedging provide suitable sheltering spots for birds. — SN

What should I do about tent caterpillars? This year, they seem to be out in full force.

There are three species of tent caterpillars native to Canada, but the two species we most commonly see in our prairie gardens are the western tent caterpillar (*Malacosoma californicum*) and the forest tent caterpillar (*M. disstria*). Both are easily identifiable. The western tent caterpillar sports a row of blue and orange spots on a reddish-brown back, while the forest tent caterpillar is black with blue and yellow stripes on its sides and white spots on its back. Tent caterpillars are approximately two inches (five centimetres) long and are covered in tiny hairs called setae, which make them appear fuzzy. The adult moth of the western tent caterpillar is orange brown in colour with some yellow flash on its wings, while the moth of the forest tent caterpillar is medium brown with a wide, darker brown band across its wings.

Adult moths lay their eggs in late summer or early autumn. A mass consisting of 150 to 350 shiny eggs is encased in a brown or grey sac that is carefully wrapped around the branches of affected trees. The sac is coated in a substance called spumaline, which is manufactured by the moths. Spumaline helps protect the larvae against freezing and drying as they overwinter. The eggs hatch in late spring (usually at the end of May or early June), and then the caterpillars get down to feeding on every green leaf they can crawl to. Tent caterpillars are seriously thorough defoliators! As befitting their common name, western tent caterpillars create webbing to form communal "tents," used as habitation and protection. Predators aren't the only thing tent caterpillars have to worry about—they also don't like the hot sun! The webs help keep them shaded and cool. The tents can be quite elaborate and even cover the tips of tree branches. Forest tent caterpillars don't make tents; instead, they create a type of mat that is used for shelter. They leave trails of silk webbing as they feed, travelling from branch to branch.

In late June or July, forest tent caterpillars will kick into high gear to complete their life cycle, creating yellow or white pupal cocoons and a goodly amount of webbing. (Western tent caterpillars go through the process a bit later in the year, closer to August.) The adult moths emerge ten days later and mate within twenty-four hours, wasting no time in laying eggs.

There are a few positive things to note about tent caterpillars: Unlike many other pest insects, they produce only one generation per year, which means that the population, while large, doesn't quite approach aphid status. Depending on factors such as the weather, outbreaks of severe tent caterpillar infestations only occur approximately every ten years, although the outbreaks themselves can last for two years. Finally, they rarely kill healthy trees, although the defoliation can slow development. If a tree is stressed or in poor health to begin with, a tent caterpillar infestation can be more troubling, as it opens the door to attacks from other pests and diseases.

Try the following methods to control tent caterpillars:

1. Look for egg casings in the spring. When you see them, scrape them from the tree, exercising extreme care not to damage the bark. Throw the cases into the garbage.
2. Later, in the summer, when you notice that the larvae are holed up in the cocoons, remove them as well, webbing and all. Dispose of them in the garbage.
3. Encourage predators to your garden. Birds, rodents, and parasitic insects such as some species of wasps love to dine on tent caterpillars. Make your garden a safe haven for these helpers. Plant a diverse range of plant species and avoid the use of pesticides.
4. If you feel you have no other option, you can employ a dormant oil spray in the early spring before your trees leaf out. You must be able to see the egg casings to do this, as the goal is to smother the eggs. If you cannot see the casings, don't waste your time and money spraying.

Some traditional advice to combat tent caterpillars involves wrapping tree trunks in aluminum foil or greasing tree bark with lard to keep the caterpillars from crawling up the trees. These methods are not recommended—save these items for use in the kitchen instead.[16]—SN

I have stink bugs in the garden. What can I do about them?

Stink bugs or shield bugs belong to a superfamily of insects, the Pentatomoidea, with some 7,000 species, and belong within the "true bugs" or Heteroptera suborder. They are easily recognizable as they have a broad shield-like covering that can be brown, green, or even black and red. They have piercing, sucking mouthparts, and if you get close enough to see them, you may notice that they have antennae divided into five segments, hence their superfamily's botanical name. Their common name comes from the fact that when threatened, they secrete a rather foul-smelling liquid to deter an attack.

For the most part, we can ignore our native species, such as the green stink bug or twice-stabbed stink bug, as they seldom cause significant damage. The one that is causing much damage and alarm is an exotic species from Asia. The brown marmorated stink bug (*Halyomorpha halys*) was introduced to North America in the 1990s and is considered a major agricultural pest. It prefers warmth, especially as the temperatures dip in the fall, and may seek a comfy home for the winter in your home. On the prairies, our winters are a natural barrier, and so far, this invasive pest has not been a huge problem.

To deter stink bugs in your garden and keep their populations in balance, encourage natural predators to your garden through a great biodiversity of plants and habitats. Tachinid flies, parasitic wasps, spiders, assassin bugs, and birds are all predators and will control stink bugs for you. Keep weeds and garden debris in check as stink bugs use them as hiding places.

There are a few deterrents if you do end up with an infestation that needs managing. Start with spraying them with water to wash them away. If they persist, spraying them with soapy water or garlic spray may be effective. Kaolin clay can be liquefied and used as a spray, which sticks to the bodies of stink bugs and suffocates them. It can also be sprayed onto vulnerable plants to deter stink bugs from feeding on them, without damage to the plants. Plant stinky plants such as marigolds, catmint, and garlic to repel stink bugs. And have a handy mint plant near doors, so the stink bugs don't come inside. Avoid turning on outside lights at night, as the bugs are attracted to both the warmth and the light. You can even

Keeping your garden weed-free helps discourage stink bugs.

grow trap plants—or, as I call them, "sacrificial lamb" plants—such as sunflowers to attract the stink bugs and keep them off the plants you value.

As always, evaluate how much of a problem stink bugs are causing before deciding on a course of action, and go with the easiest and most low-tech options first. After all, our stink bugs were with us long before we decided we could grow tomatoes on the prairies.[17] —JM

I'm seeing masses of boxelder bugs this fall! Do I need to do something about them?

Adult boxelder bugs, also called maple bugs (*Boisea trivittata*), typically congregate in the thousands once the weather begins to cool. Boxelder bugs are striking-looking insects. The adults grow about 1/2 inch (1.3 centimetres) long. Their black wings are edged with red, and a black thorax is distinctively marked with three red lines. Boxelder bugs seek the warmth and shelter of buildings to overwinter in. While they don't usually do any damage to the structures they gain access to, if they get inside your home, they may leave unwelcome gifts of excrement—not to mention that dealing with such a large population is likely to be pretty upsetting for you and your family. (Fortunately, boxelder bugs do not bite! But like their relatives, stink bugs, they release a foul-smelling chemical when crushed.)

Boxelder bugs are named after their favourite food, boxelder trees (also called Manitoba maples). They are not restricted to one type of meal; they will also feed on ash trees and other maples. Boxelder bugs have sucking mouthparts, which dig into the undersides of leaves and the seed pods of boxelder trees. This causes the leaves to exhibit white stippling on the top sides. The leaves may also turn yellow or show signs of distorted growth. The insects tend to favour female, seed-bearing boxelder trees over males. So if you wish to plant a boxelder in your garden and are worried about the threat of boxelder bugs, try to obtain a male tree.

Boxelder nymphs gather in massive numbers in the early summer, after the eggs have hatched. The nymphs are bright red in colour with a black abdomen.

The damage done to boxelder trees by their namesake insects is mostly cosmetic, and controls are not usually required. Preventing them from getting inside your house is more important: Do an annual inspection before autumn and ensure that any cracks in the building's foundation, or gaps in doors, windows, or siding, are sealed up. If you feel that chemical controls are the only solution, you can use insecticidal soap on the masses of insects. Direct contact is necessary for success. Ensure you follow all safety rules when applying pesticides, and bear in mind that the spray is non-selective and may harm insects that are not boxelder bugs. Do not spray insecticidal soap indoors.[18]—SN

My cotoneaster shrubs have oystershell scale. What can I do to combat it?

Oystershell scale (*Lepidosaphes ulmi*) is an armoured insect that is the bane of cotoneaster (*Cotoneaster* spp.) hedges, a member of the rose family, now found in so many urban areas. Oystershell scale has many hosts including other members of the rose family (Rosaceae), such as the apple (*Malus* spp.) and the hawthorn (*Crataegus* spp.); plus a number of other trees and shrubs not in the rose family, such as dogwood, willow, elm, and lilac. But it is the epidemic affecting our hedges and reducing them to ugly, dead sticks that is causing the most angst.

It is an introduced pest. Oystershell scale was first mentioned as being in Europe back in the 1700s, but it is now prevalent throughout North America. Oystershell is one of over 2,500 scale insects that can be found in the Diaspididae family. There is only one generation per year. With the female already attached to the host tree or hedge, she lays eggs underneath a protective waxy cover in late fall. The eggs hatch in late May to mid-June. In the first tiny instar stage, they are called "crawlers," as they travel over the branches before settling down to feed on the sap from the host through their mouthparts that can pierce the bark of a host and suck out sap. They mature over the summer, with the males emerging to mate with the females. After mating, the males die, but the females continue the reproductive cycle over the winter to hatch a new round of nymphs the following year.

The telltale symptom of an oystershell scale infestation is the appearance of branches covered with scales that look for all the world like crusted oyster shells. More severe infestations can lead to the death of branches, and eventually the entire hedge will die if left unchecked. More importantly, the insects will have moved on to infest other trees and shrubs on other properties.

Scale insects are difficult to control since they come with their own protection. The only time that they are particularly vulnerable is at the crawler stage, which lasts just ten days or so, roughly around late May. This stage can be very difficult to predict, and since the crawlers are so small, they are hard to spot when they hatch and start moving around. Applications of horticultural or dormant oils at exactly the right time will work to smother the nymphs and prevent furthering the infestation for the year. I have never been successful at this game, and the insects always have gone on their way unharmed!

Unwelcome as this advice is, the best way to control oystershell scale, once your hedge is infested, is to cut it right down to the ground, preferably in late winter before things start stirring. Once spring comes, the plants will quickly send up new shoots, and within a couple of years the hedge will be renewed.

Most shrubs should be pruned every year with the removal of up to 20 percent of the branches to ensure the plant is kept vigorous. Mature hedges that have been in place for years and are trimmed only to make them neat become old and stressed and are prime candidates for an infestation. It doesn't help that in many urban areas cotoneaster hedges are almost a monoculture, so there is no lack of hosts for this scale insect.

Once your hedge has been cut to the ground, bag up the branches and dispose of them in the garbage. Then turn your attention to providing the best conditions for the rejuvenating hedge. Ensure that weeds and encroaching grass are removed from around the stems. Add compost and other soil amendments to enrich the soil, and make sure the hedge is well watered on a regular basis. Once the hedge is well established again, make sure to remove the oldest branches on a five-year cycle to keep renewing the plant's vigour. Finally, monitor for any signs of oystershell scale insects making a reappearance, especially if there are other hedges in the neighbourhood that are affected. Scale insects fly as adults, particularly the males in search of the females.

We often view our hedges as background plants, and don't provide the necessary care to ensure they stay healthy. Once we change that view and see them as beautiful, hardy, and purposeful plants in the garden to be well cared for, then we will see a reduction in the populations of scale insects and the resulting infestations.[19] —JM

Oystershell scale can quickly ravage a cotoneaster hedge.

How do I combat elm scale?

The life cycle and habits of European elm scale (EES) insects (*Eriococcus spurius*) are fascinating, but the creatures are universally detested by gardeners and urban foresters alike. Elms are a common boulevard and yard tree on the prairies (for good reason—they are hardy for our climate and extremely beautiful!), but, due to this monoculture of plantings, EES insects have gotten a substantial foothold over the past few decades. Cumulatively, EES infestations over several years can slowly cause the health of elm trees to decline, even promoting branch dieback.

EES insects have sucking mouthparts, which they use to extract juices from the leaves of elm trees. It is easy to overlook the insects until the trees start putting out distress signals, and by then, the infestation may be serious. Look for yellowing or browning of leaves, or leaf drop in the summer, instead of in the autumn. Branches may brown and die. Telltale symptoms are if you find yourself sprayed

This elm has a serious case of sooty mould, caused by the honeydew produced by elm scale insects.

with a mysterious substance when you walk by your elm tree, or if you see drips on your sidewalk or driveway near the tree. In addition to causing feeding damage, elm scale insects also produce honeydew (truthfully: it's insect pee!). The honeydew may attract ants. The ants do not harm the trees, but may attack parasitoid insects that target EES insects. The honeydew also promotes the formation of sooty mould, which causes the tree bark to turn black.

EES nymphs overwinter in the branches of trees. The males and females pupate at different times early in spring, but when they emerge, mating typically takes place in May. Females lay eggs in batches over a period of about six weeks. The eggs hatch quickly—sometimes just an hour after they are laid! During this period, the females continue to feed on the limbs of trees. They are easy to spot with their characteristic hard fringed body armour. The females die once all of their eggs are laid, but their scales may persist on the host tree. The newly hatched nymphs begin as tiny wormlike crawlers, focused on eating leaves. By late August or early September, they head for the safety of the tree branches to prepare for winter.[20]

Elm trees that are stressed from extreme heat, drought, mechanical damage (for example, due to someone running a lawn mower into the trunk), or other pests and infections are easy targets for elm scale insects. Offer your elm tree the very best care you can, so that it can fight off attacks. Site it properly when you plant it, giving it space to grow and good soil to do it in. Fulfill its needs regarding water and nutrients, and keep up with tasks such as weeding around the base and pruning out dead wood. (Remember that there are provincial restrictions on pruning green, live limbs and branches on elm trees to help prevent another serious threat to elm trees, Dutch elm disease. Consult with your local and provincial governments to determine which months it is safe to prune elms.)[21]

If you find that your elm tree is infested year after year with EES, and you fear for its health, your options for treatments are slim. There are some parasitoid insects being employed as biological controls in some parts of North America, but they are not available for home garden use on the Canadian prairies. You can try applying a horticultural oil just before the buds blossom or in the early autumn to try to get rid of overwintering nymphs. If you can see the scale insects on the tree, you can gently wipe them off the bark with gloved hands—but, of course, this is impossible to do if your tree is mature.

Pest control companies use systemic insecticides to deal with EES; the chemicals are injected directly into the tree at any time throughout the growing season.—SN

The leaves on my plants look like the insides have been "tunnelled" through. What could this be from?

This sort of damage is caused by leaf miners. Birch trees are often affected, but most plants, from annual flowers and vegetables, to herbaceous and woody perennials, are susceptible. So . . . everything from aspens to zinnias, then!

There are several categories of leaf-mining insects, and each one has a preferred diet. Birch leaf miners (*Fenusa pumila*) are flies that happily chow down on all species of birch trees (as well as alders). Other leaf miners may be moths,

What are horticultural and dormant oils and should I use them? If so, when?

Horticultural and dormant oils are usually petroleum-based pesticides, used to control insects (and some diseases) on plants. There are some plant-based oils as well, made from soybeans, sesame, or neem, but the petroleum oils are usually preferred because they are more refined and less likely to burn plants if used properly. Horticultural oils are often used to control scale insects, aphids, and leafhoppers, among others. Some diseases, such as leaf spot and powdery mildew, may be treated with horticultural oils.

Dormant oil is a term that refers to a horticultural oil that is used only when the plant is dormant (before the buds open in the spring). Dormant oils only work to combat insects that are overwintering on the plant or that may have laid visible eggs on the surface of the plant.

Other oils may be applied after the buds have blossomed, although they are generally more effective against insects that do not have hard exoskeletons. Time application to attack eggs or the immature, soft-bodied juveniles. The oil must be in direct contact with the insect eggs or bodies to work. Bear in mind that any insects the oil touches may be suffocated—the treatment is non-selective and beneficial creatures may be harmed. The oils are no longer effective when they dry up, however, so they do not leave toxic residue.

Be sure to attempt other controls, such as hand-picking the insects off the tree, before deciding to break out the horticultural oils. If you do choose to use the oils, carefully follow the instructions on the package and wear protective clothing. Horticultural oils can burn plants if applied improperly. (Conifers are particularly susceptible to this.)[22]

Leaf miner insects feed on cells between leaf layers.

sawflies, or beetles. Although the timing of their life cycles varies, leaf miner insects typically lay eggs on or inside leaves, giving the larvae a head start on feeding as soon as they hatch. The larvae munch on the leaf cells between the layers of the leaves, creating distinct tunnels where the juices have been removed. If you take a look at an affected leaf while the larva is active, you'll actually see (or feel) the body between the top and the underside of the leaf. The mined leaves may brown and curl at the edges, due to the loss of fluids. Sometimes you'll also notice small bits of black frass collected on the leaves. Leaf miners prefer leaves that appear on new shoots, so if you pruned heavily the previous year, your plant may be more susceptible.

Once each larva has had its fill and is fully grown, it enters the pupal stage, building a cocoon in the foliage or in the soil at the base of the plant. The timing of adult emergence varies depending on the type of insect. The adults immediately mate, and the females search for egg-laying real estate. There may be more than one generation of insects per year. Reproduction is determined by species and weather conditions. Leaf miners are not fazed by prairie winters and will successfully ride them out underground.

Several native and non-native parasitoid wasps and predator insects attack leaf miners; the best way to control leaf miners is to let these beneficials do their jobs! The damage is mostly cosmetic and doesn't usually do significant damage to mature plants (although the health of young or previously stressed plants may be compromised). Contact pesticides are not recommended—they will not hurt leaf-mining insects while they are feeding, as the larvae are protected by the surfaces of the leaves.[23]—SN

There is usually no need to take action if you see evidence of leafroller activity on your trees.

My aspen trees are infested with little white worms that are curled up inside rolled leaves. Is there anything I can do?

There are several types of leafroller moths, most native to North America. They are thusly named because the larvae love to feed and pupate inside rolled up leaves. The rolls are easily identifiable and are tied together with webbing that the larva has manufactured. (Sometimes the larva will nestle itself, sandwich-like, between two leaves and fuse them together instead of making a roll.) Individual species of leafrollers tend to feast on one or more preferred types of host plant; for example, *Archips purpurana* is particularly fond of aspen, willow, and birch trees. Other leafrollers may feed on plants such as saskatoon berry, apple, cherry, ash, and elm trees. Newly emerged leaves are much favoured over developed ones. During a severe infestation, leafrollers can do quite a lot of damage by reducing the amount of leaf surface in the trees, thus minimizing the tree's ability to photosynthesize.

Leafrollers have several enemies, including tachinid flies and some parasitoid wasps, which target the larvae. Predator insects such as lacewings and assassin bugs are also fond of leafroller larvae. Birds may also feed on leafrollers. Most of the time, these biological controls can restrict the population of leafrollers, and no help from the gardener is required. The problem is truly more cosmetic than anything.

If you absolutely feel you need to treat the problem, and you see exposed egg masses on plants, hose them off with strong blasts of water from the garden hose or wipe them off with gloved hands and dispose of them. Application of pesticides while the insects are in their feeding or pupating stage is not useful, as they are protected by their leafy hotel rooms. If you are not averse to using chemicals and feel you have no other choice, you can try to diminish the number of eggs that will hatch by using a horticultural oil before the trees' buds open. Be sure to follow all package instructions and wear any protective clothing needed during application.[24]—SN

Little white worms are eating my onions. What should I do?

If your onions begin yellowing and flopping over during midsummer, well before the bulbs are ready to harvest, pull one up to take a look. The leaves will likely separate from the bulb, and if you dig the bulb up, it will probably be rotten and hollow. You may even see the culprits: small white legless larvae called onion maggots. One of the worst things about onion maggots is that you rarely notice them until after they've fed on your onions underground, ruining them. The adult flies resemble small grey houseflies, so you wouldn't likely remark on them.[25]

Adult flies emerge from overwintered pupae in late spring and early summer. Each female lays up to 200 eggs, near the stalks of onions or in the folds of leaves, positioned so that the larvae do not have to crawl far to find food. The eggs take approximately ten days to hatch. The larvae feed for up to three weeks, travelling from bulb to bulb.

On the prairies, onion maggot flies are capable of producing two generations per year. The second generation, hatched from adults that emerge at the end of summer and early autumn, overwinter as pupae in the soil. The second generation usually does not do as much feeding damage to onion plants as the first generation does, but you may still be hesitant to eat the bulbs, as they may be soft, and they will likely rot in storage.

Try these methods to prevent and control onion maggots:

1. Position yellow sticky tape traps near your onion plants to trap flying adults.
2. Onion maggots love to lay their eggs in damp, heavily fertile soil. If you're worried about maggots, hold back a bit of water and nutrients for this crop.
3. Put up floating row covers to discourage the adult flies from getting too up close and personal with your onion plants. Because there are two generations of maggots, the row covers must remain in place all season.

4. Rotate onion crops annually.

5. After harvest, clean up all debris from onion plants. This will hopefully remove resting pupae intending to overwinter.[26]

—SN

Onion maggots can be an unwelcome surprise at harvest time.

Dill is an excellent insectary plant—plus, you'll love its culinary uses!

What are the best insectary plants for the prairies?

Insectary plants are deliberately grown to provide food and shelter for parasitoid insects and other types of insect predators such as lacewings, ladybugs, hoverflies, *Trichogramma* wasps, and tachinid flies. Insectary plants typically provide nectar and pollen, and therefore may also, as a bonus, attract pollinating insects. The goal of planting insectary plants is to build a population of pest predators and, in doing so, provide cultivated garden plants with biological controls.

When choosing insectary plants, look for those that have long, staggered, and overlapping blooming periods, so that they go strong all season. Bear in mind that you cannot simply "plant 'em and leave 'em"—insectary plants will need as much maintenance as the crop and ornamental plants they are helping to protect. Ensure they have sufficient water, nutrients, and sunlight for their needs. Site them in locations where they will thrive, with appropriate soil conditions and proper drainage. Insectary plants are often planted in the perimeter of a vegetable or ornamental garden, but they may also be very effectively interplanted among the cultivated crops. Don't skimp on the numbers—and diversity—of insectary plants you put in your garden, as the insects they attract will hang around longer if they have enough food and safe habitat to thrive.

Try these insectary plants to bring the "beneficials" to your yard!

HERBACEOUS PERENNIALS:
Basket-of-gold (*Alyssum saxatilis*)
Bugleweed (*Ajuga reptans*)
Feverfew (*Tanacetum parthenium*)
Goldenrod (*Solidago canadensis*)
    and related species and cultivars
Lamb's ears (*Stachys byzantina*)
Masterwort (*Astrantia major*)
Speedwell (*Veronica spicata*)
Wild bergamot (*Monarda fistulosa*)
Wood betony (*Stachys officinalis*)
Yarrow (*Achillea millefolium*)

ANNUALS—TENDER PERENNIALS:
Calendula (*Calendula officinalis*)
Cosmos (*Cosmos bipinnatus*)
Golden marguerite (*Anthemis tinctoria*)
'Lemon Gem' and 'Orange Gem'
marigold (*Tagetes tenuifolia*)
Phacelia (*Phacelia tanacetifolia*)
Prairie sunflower (*Helianthus maximiliani*)
Sweet alyssum (*Lobularia maritima*)
Zinnia (*Zinnia elegans*)

HERBS—MEMBERS OF THE CARROT FAMILY (APIACEAE):
Coriander (*Coriandrum sativum*)
Dill (*Anethum graveolens*)
Fennel (*Foeniculum vulgare*)
Lovage (*Levisticum officinale*)
Parsley (*Petroselinum crispum*)

PLUS SOME OTHER HERBS TO CONSIDER:
Caraway (*Carum carvi*)
Dandelion (*Taraxacum officinale*)
English lavender (*Lavandula angustifolia*)
Lemon balm (*Melissa officinalis*)
Thyme (*Thymus spp.*)[27]

Bacteria, Fungi, Viruses, and Other Micro-organisms

3

ABOVE: *These caragana leaves are afflicted with powdery mildew.*

LEFT: *Some types of squash have white-spotted foliage that gardeners may mistake for powdery mildew. There is nothing wrong with these plants— the colouration of the leaves is natural.*

Powdery mildew: My plants are covered with a white powdery substance! What is it and how do I control it?

Powdery mildew is a disease caused by a species of fungus in the order Erysiphales. Many of these mildews are species specific, meaning that if one type of plant in your garden is affected, other species may not be at risk. For all intents and purposes, the fungi that cause powdery mildew are always within the environment, but need the right conditions to really take off and be a problem. So some years are worse than others, literally depending on the weather that year. What these fungi really like are damp (not wet) and/or higher-humidity conditions and moderately warm temperatures, but not lots of heat or rain.

We cannot control the weather, but we can help to manage our gardens, so that powdery mildews do not become a problem. The key is to make sure that all plants have lots of air circulation. Closely spaced plants are the perfect environment for the fungi to flourish in. Learn which plants in your garden are prone to mildew and monitor for early signs. An easy homemade preventive is a baking soda solution sprayed weekly on the tops and bottoms of plant leaves. Baking soda has a high pH value, so it creates an environment not hospitable to fungus species. If you do see powdery mildew, try a diluted milk solution, sprayed onto the leaves once every two weeks. Scientists are not really sure why it works to control the fungus, but it does!

When a plant is infected, prune off the worst of the affected leaves and dispose of them in the garbage. New growth should be free of the disease and grow strongly if you ensure the plant is as healthy as possible and watch for further signs of powdery mildew on the new leaves. In the fall, clean up and dispose of all leaves, preferably in the garbage, as the fungi can overwinter in leaf debris. As a last resort, if a plant is so severely infected that it is not likely to recover, pull it out and dispose of it quickly. There is always next year when you may be able to choose a mildew-resistant variety of the plant you had tried to grow or something else that is not susceptible to mildew. —JM

Black knot: My tree has a lumpy black growth on its branches! What is it? How do I treat it?

If your tree or shrub is of the *Prunus* genus that includes cherry, plum, choke-cherry, Amur maple, or mayday species, chances are that the plant has been infected by the fungus *Apiosporina morbosa*, commonly known as black knot. While all species in the genus are susceptible to the fungus, mayday, Schubert chokecherry, and native chokecherries are the ones where the fungus is the most aggressive and have been the hardest hit in recent years, with some calling the situation an epidemic. Unfortunately, in Alberta, our love of both the mayday and Schubert chokecherries, combined with some cool and wet springs a few years ago, were perfect conditions for the fungus to become endemic. It is hard these days to walk down an urban street and not see just about every tree affected to some degree, or stroll in a wild area and not see all our native chokecherry shrubs bearing the telltale black knobby growths on their branches, stems, or trunks.

There is no cure or treatment for plants that have become infected. You can only mitigate the situation by pruning, so knowledge of how the fungus works and good cultural techniques are key to keeping your plants healthy.

The fungus spreads by way of ascospores that grow on the surface of the cankers and are released in the spring after a mild period of rainy and windy weather. If the plant is of a species that is a host to the fungus, a small olive-green gall will develop at the site of infection. The gall will slowly grow over several years and turn black. As the galls increase in size, they girdle the tree branches and trunk.

To try to prolong the lives of diseased trees, prune out all knots on the branches during the late fall, winter, or early spring. Cut at least six to eight inches (fifteen to twenty centimetres) below the knots. Do not leave branch stubs. The infected plant parts must not be composted. Look to your municipality's regulations regarding disposal in your area.

Minimize the stress on your *Prunus* trees by sticking to a consistent watering schedule throughout the growing season. A side dressing of compost once per year, in the spring, may be useful.[1] —JM

If your tree belongs to the genus Prunus *and it is sporting growths like this, you'll need to get out the pruning tools.*

The foliage on my aspens is turning orange red in colour. What could be the issue?

The problem is likely bronze leaf disease (BLD). Caused by the fungus *Apioplagiostoma populi*, BLD affects only trees of the genus *Populus*. These include the Swedish columnar aspen (*Populus tremula* 'Erecta'), the tower poplar (*Populus × canescens* 'Tower'), trembling aspen (*Populus tremuloides*), and others.

Watch for signs of BLD in late summer. Leaves will suddenly, over only a few days, turn bronze or reddish orange in colour in late August or early September. The leaf veins will initially remain bright green while the rest of the leaf discolours; eventually, the veins will turn black. (Remember that poplar leaves normally turn yellow, not bronze, in the fall.) You may notice the bronzing on only a few branches, not on the whole tree. The bronze leaves will not usually fall to the ground, but will stay on the tree over the winter.

The spores of *A. populi* will spread rapidly via the wind to other nearby poplars. The warm temperatures and precipitation during the following spring will accelerate spore bloom.

In the growing seasons following the initial infection, the lower branches will brown and die. Before they waste away, the branches will continue to leaf out in the spring. The foliage will be green at that time, but the leaves may be smaller than those on unaffected branches, and they will turn bronze in the fall. It will take time, but if left untreated, the fungus will eventually girdle the entire tree.

Controlling BLD is tricky and—we're not going to lie—sometimes feels a bit futile. The best option is to prune out the affected branches. Cut to a branch collar for best results, or to the trunk if absolutely required. Sanitize your pruning tools between cuts, using a solution of one part bleach to ten parts water. The diseased branches must not be composted—it is best to bag them and send them to your local landfill.

Practice good Integrated Pest Management by monitoring trees for signs of disease or other problems that may arise due to stress. Minimize the risk of multiple or secondary infections or infestations. Water and fertilize as recommended, and prune regularly to open up air circulation in the crown of your trees.

Finally, if your aspens or poplars have BLD, clean up all of the leaf litter beneath the trees in the autumn. Usually it is good practice to leave leaf litter for use as mulch during the winter, but this is not the time to do so, as the leaves may contain spores of A. *populi*.

If you are planning to plant any poplar species in your yard, do not plant them too closely to one another, as that could facilitate the spread of BLD spores. Promote biodiversity in your garden by planting several different species of trees instead of just one type.[2] —SN

My potatoes are scabby. What can I do to prevent this for next year?

Scab is caused by *Streptomyces scabies*, a bacterium-like organism that is widespread and prevalent on the prairies, due to our alkaline soils. The tubers will have lesions on the surface that look for all the world like the kind of scabs we get on our skin after we have been injured. The good news is that while scab looks unsightly, you can just peel it off, and the rest of the potato is perfectly fine to eat.

The bad news is that the organism not only can live in soil for many years, but also will affect other root crops, in the absence of potatoes, making effective crop rotation complicated to nearly impossible in the average garden.

As with all problems affecting what we grow, understanding the disease triangle pays dividends. Scab is our pathogen, and we can assume that it is always present, as not only does it reside in soil for years, but it can appear in other areas of the garden, transported by wind or rain. Scab can also be present in infected tubers that you purchase, or ones saved from the previous season.

The host is usually potatoes, but it can also be found in beets, parsnips, and all root brassicas. Many potato varieties, including rough-skinned cultivars like 'Russet Burbank', have been bred to be resistant to scab, while others, including the thin-skinned varieties such as 'Yukon Gold', are known to be susceptible. Look for 'Norland', 'Dakota Pearl', 'Chieftain', and other varieties that are rated to have moderate to good resistance to scab. To avoid introducing scab into your garden, always purchase certified seed potatoes from sources you trust.

The trick then is to make the third angle of the triangle, the environmental conditions, less favourable to the pathogen. Scab flourishes in dry alkaline soils that are moist but not wet, and that are low in organic matter. Growing a cover crop, such as sowing rye in the fall, or sowing alfalfa or mustard greens in the spring, then tilling it into the soil three weeks before planting, will add necessary biomass and many nutrients needed for potatoes to thrive. Adding elemental sulphur or peat moss will act to buffer the pH of slightly alkaline soils. Most vegetables prefer neutral to slightly acidic soils, so this action will not be detrimental to other edibles grown in successive years. Clay-based soils benefit from the addition of gypsum, which not only acts to improve soil texture, but also adds calcium. This helps build strong cellular walls in plants, which then can better resist the pathogen that interferes with good cellular wall development. (The scabs are the plant's visible response to the presence of the pathogen.) Do ensure that the soil is consistently moist, especially after the plants flower and early tuber formation occurs. Moist soil is conducive to good soil life, and the goal is to encourage good bacteria that will crowd out the bacteria that cause scab. Not to mention that to have good tuber formation, good soil moisture is essential.

Finally, we recommend practising crop rotation. Potatoes should not be planted in successive years in the same bed. Absence of the host will act to reduce populations of the pathogen. Look for other places to plant your potatoes, other than in the bed you have previously used, such as grow bags and potato towers. Sometimes the unlikeliest places will produce the best results, as I discovered when I found potatoes growing in my compost pile. They were the tastiest and best-formed potatoes, with not a trace of scab to be found. When you think of it, your compost pile is consistently moist and full of organic matter, and has a neutral pH. No wonder those potatoes were the best![3]—JM

Try planting resistant varieties to thwart the disease that causes the knobby growths on these potatoes.

I am noticing blackening and girdling on some of the stems of my apple trees. What is this?

This saskatoon shrub exhibits the characteristic blackening and shepherd's-crook form of fire blight.

Fire blight is caused by a bacterium (*Erwinia amylovora*) that affects members of the rose family, including hawthorn, saskatoon berry, plum, pear, mountain ash, and cotoneaster. Orchard owners and fruit tree growers are particularly concerned with this problem, as it can seriously affect crops such as apples and crabapples. The bacteria are transmitted from plant to plant by insects, wind, and water (either by rain or by irrigation). A humid, wet spring and consistently warm temperatures promote the spread of the pathogen.

Infected branches and leaves will look burnt and turn black, but the leaves will not fall off the tree, not even during the following winter. The tips of the twigs will curl over in what is termed a "shepherd's crook." (If you don't see the crooks, you are probably not dealing with fire blight.) Eventually, the bark on the infected branches will blacken and form cankers. The cankers are dark rough patches that may be cracked at the edges. They are filled with bacteria, which sometimes oozes down tree limbs and attracts flies and other insects. If left unchecked, the cankers will girdle the branches and cause dieback of entire sections of the tree. The bacteria may also cause some blooms to brown. (This is called blossom blight.) It may even attack the rootstock or collars of grafted trees.[4] If fire blight takes hold of tree trunks and root systems, the tree is not likely to survive. The cankers are not affected by our harsh winters.

84

One of the interesting (and frightening!) things about fire blight is how quickly, under warm and humid conditions, the bacteria can multiply. The population can double in just a few hours! If you think about the thousands of fire blight cells a single fly can pick up, or the wind can blow around, the potential for a serious outbreak is alarming.

Another scary fact is that fire blight bacteria don't live only in cankers on an affected tree. The bacteria may also live as epiphytes, and can be found in what looks like healthy tissues, including flowers and branches. In other words, you'll never know the blight is there!

If possible, choose fire blight–resistant cultivars when shopping for trees. This information will usually be indicated on the plant label, but you may have to do some research beforehand.

Do not overfertilize your trees, especially with high-nitrogen fertilizer. Fire blight loves to attack succulent, lush green growth. To prevent shoot blight, prune away any watershoots or suckers from trees, as these new growths are sites the bacteria prefer to infect first.

Any branches that have grown cankers should be pruned away in the late fall or early spring. If you can, cut back at least twelve inches (thirty centimetres) below the canker into the healthy wood. Don't forget to disinfect your pruning shears between cuts with a solution of bleach and water. Keep your gloves and hands clean as well, so you do not spread the bacteria. Infected branches must not be composted.[5] — SN

My junipers have masses of orange gelatinous goo in them. What is this and what can I do about it?

The bright orange blobs that can be seen on junipers and cedars in spring are a sign of a fungal species of rust, endemic in western Canada, that requires two hosts to propagate. They include: cedar-apple rust (*Gymnosporangium juniperi-virginianae*), cedar-hawthorn rust (*G. globosum*), and cedar-quince rust (*G. clavipes*).

These gelatinous masses are exuded from mature galls on either juniper or cedar trees during warm and wet springs. They go on to develop telia (hornlike extrusions) that release spores in the wind, which then land on the leaves of one of many alternate hosts for the fungi in the botanical order Rosales, such as apple, pear, hawthorn, mountain ash, saskatoon, rose, and cotoneaster. Lesions appear on the leaves of the alternate host shortly after blooming, looking like small round orange spots. Occasionally, in severe infestations, the lesions can be seen on the fruit, which causes either premature drop or, if the fruit remains on the plant, is of poor quality or is not edible. Over especially hot and wet summers, little tubes from the undersides of the leaves, called aecia, develop and release spores that then infect the host plant. The infected juniper or cedar grows brown galls the following spring. It takes another year for the galls to mature and go on to create another round of infection.

The good news is that the presence of this rust does not seriously stress or harm either the host or the alternate host. The alternate host's leaves can still perform photosynthesis, so the impact is minimal unless the incidence is severe over successive years.

Being an endemic and native fungal species, this fungus is always with us, but it is more evident when the weather is just right, creating ideal conditions for the spores to disseminate, infect the host and alternate host, and mature to complete the cycle. In some years with drier conditions, there are few signs of the fungus in either host.

While the galls can be unsightly to some eyes—although as a gardener, I am fascinated by them—there is little point in pruning them away. As it takes the proximity of both host and alternate host for the fungi to survive, the usual advice

This juniper is affected by rust.

is to refrain from planting them in the same garden. In an urban environment where many gardeners are creating their own gardens, this is often impractical advice since there are multitudes of trees and shrubs already well established.

Planting rust-resistant species will assist in reducing the numbers of hosts, so if you live in an area prone to periodic infestations, check out the profile of the variety you are considering and try to find one that is not prone to rust.

There are fungicides available to treat rust, but they require a pesticide operator's licence to use, and, as with all pesticides, they may have a negative impact on other plants and creatures in the garden and should be used only as the final threshold of response.[6] —JM

The leaves on my hollyhocks are blistered and discoloured. What is this caused by?

Hollyhock rust (*Puccinia heterospora*) is a fungus that is specific to members of the *Alcea* genus, which includes hollyhocks.

Triggered by hot and humid weather, overwintering spores in the soil will infect leaves and look like tiny yellow spots. The undersides of the leaves will develop pustules that look like blisters, which are the fruiting bodies. When mature, they will release reddish-brown spores that can coat the undersides of the leaves. Leaves will turn grey or brown and prematurely drop.

To control the fungus, remove leaves at the first sign of rust developing and dispose of them in the garbage. If a plant is severely affected, cut it down, and remove it as a source of infection. Cultural controls include: removing weeds, especially mallow plants that may harbour the fungus; watering the base of the plants to avoid splashing onto the leaves; mulching to prevent spores in the soil from emerging in the spring; thinning plants to give greater air circulation; cutting back plants at the end of the season; and removing all plant debris.

Older heirloom varieties of hollyhock are more susceptible to rust. If you have had infestations, choose cultivars that have been bred with resistance to rust, or consider removing hollyhocks from your garden for a few years. If the host is removed, then the fungus will not survive. Then reintroduce hollyhocks back into the garden, perhaps choosing another location for the new plants.[7]—JM

How can I identify and treat cytospora canker?

Have you noticed that your conifer has dark wounds dripping with white resin, and the lower branches are browning and dropping needles? Your tree may be suffering from a type of cytospora canker, a result of an infection of the fungal pathogen *Cytospora leucostoma*. Colorado blue spruce, white spruce, Norway spruce, Engelmann spruce, Douglas fir, and larch are most commonly affected. The spores of cytospora canker are released throughout the growing season and are rapidly dispersed via wind, rain, insects, birds, and even human activity. Mature trees and those that are already stressed by factors such as high heat and drought are most affected. If trees are planted closely together, the fungus can easily spread.

Poplars and willows may be afflicted by cytospora canker as well, caused by the fungal pathogen *C. chrysosperma*. In the case of poplars and willows, mostly young trees are affected; again, the canker usually attacks trees that are already stressed. Cytospora canker in poplars and willows is identifiable by dark oozing lesions (cankers) and branch dieback, due to girdling.

To slow the progress of cytospora canker, attempt the following controls:

1. Offer trees consistent, even moisture throughout the growing season. Bear in mind that too much water can have a detrimental effect on trees, suffocating and rotting root systems and stressing the tree.
2. Do not disturb root systems of trees by digging near them.
3. Do not injure tree bark. This can easily happen when you are mowing the adjacent lawn or using the grass trimmer, so exercise caution. Wounds provide a way for the fungus to enter the tree.
4. Do not prune trees when conditions are wet, as this promotes the spread of fungal spores.
5. If you see cytospora canker, remove the branch four to six inches (ten to fifteen centimetres) below the site of the wound. If you have to cut back to the trunk, do so.

6. Site trees in optimum locations, according to their individual needs. This may seem obvious, but putting a tree that loves sunlight in a deeply shaded area isn't doing it any favours, nor is offering a tree that doesn't need a lot of water the boggiest spot in your yard. In addition to ensuring they have the proper sun exposure and soil conditions, give trees the space and the air circulation they need, and supply nutrients and water as required.

7. Ensure your tree is hardy to your climate. Borderline hardy trees don't always have the ability to fight infections.[8]—SN

If a soilborne disease has killed one of my plants, can I plant something else in its place? Do I have to sterilize the soil or wait until the next year to plant in the same area?

Be they native or introduced organisms, diseases caused by bacteria, fungi, viruses, and other organisms are always in the environment.

Many overwinter in the soil or in plant debris, rather than in or on the plant. For example, black spot (*Diplocarpon rosae*) on roses overwinters beneath the plant and emerges in the spring. The fungus black knot (*Apiosporina morbosa*) is not soilborne, but rather overwinters in swellings on the host plant.

Some of these organisms can persist in the soil for decades while others will die off within a short time if they do not have a host readily available. Scab (*Streptomyces scabies*), caused by a bacterium-like organism, can remain in the soil for a long time, whereas soft-rot bacteria (*Pectobacterium carotovorum*) are not as long-lived.

Some organisms are highly specific to what kind of host they need, while others behave more like generalists. Soft-rot bacteria are generalists, whereas black knot is specific to just a few species within the genus *Prunus*.

The disease triangle provides the three steps to consider regarding how any organism may affect what we want to grow. The first angle is the organism; the second is the host (e.g., the plant in question); and the third is the environment, specifically the conditions necessary for a problem to occur. To manage the likelihood of a problem, simply remove one of the three cornerstones.

The key to a successful course of action is to correctly identify the pathogen causing the disease and know its life cycle, as well as its host and potential hosts. Often removing a host is the best solution. Also, proactively practising crop rotation for both agricultural and horticultural crops is recommended, regardless of whether there is a problem or not. If the plant in question is a permanent one, such as a tree, shrub, or forb (herbaceous perennial), then the decision can be heartbreaking. Mayday (*Prunus padus*) trees are beautiful and have many functions in our prairie gardens, but many are infected with black knot and are dying at epidemic proportions in Calgary.

Once a plant has died or been removed, you do not need to sterilize the soil. It is impractical given that organisms will repopulate the soil in short order, arriving by wind and water, and with animals and insects. Rather than attempting to replant the same plant, such as a mayday or chokecherry tree, choose a plant that provides the same functions but will not be a host to the organism. For instance, a Japanese tree lilac is not a host to black knot and can be a good substitute. Incidentally, black knot is a native fungus, but has become such a problem because so many of its hosts have been planted in our urban environment.

Environmental factors that provide the right conditions for disease-causing organisms to flourish are often the hardest to manage. Simply put, we cannot control our overall climate or weather conditions in any given year. Most fungi, bacteria, and viruses flourish in warm and humid weather. Likewise, it is difficult to permanently alter the natural pH of soils, be they acidic or alkaline, nor is it desirable as some of these organisms prefer alkaline soils and some acidic ones. Solve the pH factor for one disease, and you may encourage another to proliferate.

What we can do is ensure that our gardens are healthy and that our plants enjoy as stress-free an environment as possible, so that they are able to use their own natural defences to ward off an infestation. Do clean up plant debris, especially if it is diseased. Good hygiene goes a long way toward removing potential sources of infestations. We recommend using mulch, but no more than necessary, so that water applied to plants does not splash back up into the foliage. If there is a specific plant with a specific organism affecting it, then do apply a thicker layer of mulch locally around that plant. My yellow rose with black spot has a nice thick layer of wood chips around it, which is helping incrementally to cut back the amount of black spot over time. The rose is a tough one, and, though weakened, is still surviving and flowering.

Do amend soil regularly with compost, which adds organic matter to buffer the normal pH of your soil. In some instances, you may want to alter the pH to avoid an outbreak. Adding elemental sulphur to soil before growing potatoes is a good choice to help control scab. Another option would be to grow potatoes in containers using soil that has never grown potatoes before. Some soilborne organisms can be managed by applications of remedies, such as Bordeaux mixture, diluted milk, diluted baking soda, garlic spray, horticultural oils, and so forth. Many of these remedies can be made by the gardener using common household ingredients, with many specific recipes available online. Alternatively, similar preparations can be found at local garden centres. They won't cure the problem but may prevent one occurring, or at least keep it down to a manageable level. Finally, consider planting disease-resistant varieties when there is a known problem that may erupt given the right conditions.[9] —JM

Diseases, pathogens, symptoms, signs: What exactly do we mean by these terms?

In the simplest terms, a disease is something that disrupts the normal processes of plant development. Diseases can be caused by living (biotic) factors, such as fungi, bacteria, viruses, and even parasitic plants. Environmental conditions, such as weather, temperature, nutrient deficiency, and soil conditions, are considered factors of abiotic disease.

Pathogens, such as fungi, bacteria, and viruses, are biotic agents of disease.

Symptoms are the visible effects of disease on plants, such as distortion or spots on leaves or blackening of plant tissues (necrosis).

Signs are the actual physical evidence of pathogens on plants: powdery mildew, for example, or fungal spores.[10]

Furred, Winged, Hoofed (and Slimy!): Other Pest Critters

4

Slugs: Is it possible to get rid of them?

The first thing to keep in mind about slugs on the prairies is that they are minuscule compared to the ones I have seen on Vancouver Island! The other thing to do is to keep perspective; they are food for lots of predators, including birds, ground beetles, frogs, and even those pesky squirrels.

That said, we don't necessarily want to offer up our tender plants to their stomachs. Prevention being the best course of action, make sure to provide space between plants, so that their canopy doesn't create the perfect, humid, moist, and safe-from-predatory-eyes environment for slugs to munch away. Then regularly clean up any decaying foliage in the beds. A sharp-edged mulch will also deter them, with diatomaceous earth being a good choice, but it does need to be renewed often. Home remedies can include dried and crushed eggshells or coffee grounds. Copper mesh is known to be effective as the slugs will create an electrical charge as they attempt to cross the barrier, but it is expensive so it is best reserved for that really prized hosta.

Slugs like sweet, smooth-textured plants over those that are acrid, bitter, or rough textured. Try companion planting with species in the onion or cabbage families. Many herbs are also good deterrents.

Luring slugs to a trap is another strategy, with beer often being touted as the best substance to use. Even easier is yeast, as it is the yeast in beer, not the alcohol, that attracts them. Be sure to replace it regularly. Since slugs are nocturnal, other gardeners we know will go out at night with a flashlight and sprinkle salt on those that they find.

If all this seems like a lot of work, then do what we do: Keep your garden beds open with good air circulation, then ignore the slugs and the damage they do. Consider it a trade-off for the benefits they provide for our prairie environment. After all, we are not on Vancouver Island! — JM

*Regular nighttime sojourns to sprinkle salt
and leave offerings of beer will help deplete
the numbers of these voracious herbivores.*

What can I do to prevent ticks in my yard?

Keeping ticks away from you, your family, and your pets is important, as these parasitic arthropods can be vectors of disease in humans and animals. Ticks love to hang out in the tall grass or thickly wooded areas at the edges of lawns and yards. Areas that are damp and shady are also attractive to them.

Take the following steps to minimize contact with ticks:

1. Do not allow your lawn to become shaggy. Mow frequently.
2. Create a gravel barrier between your lawn and any nearby wooded areas. Ticks don't like crawling over rough dry surfaces.
3. Remove any debris such as old furniture and mattresses from the yard.
4. If ticks are prevalent in the area, clean up fallen leaves and fruit, as well as pruned branches.
5. It's easier said than done, but try to discourage animals that attract ticks (and may bring them into your yard). We're looking at you, deer.
6. Wear protective clothing when you are outside working in the garden. Put on long-sleeved shirts tucked into pants, as well as socks and boots or closed-toe shoes. A hat is also a good idea. Spray clothing and skin with DEET if you are not averse to using this chemical.
7. Do a tick check after leaving the garden! Have someone help you, so you don't miss any areas. Don't forget to check your pets as well. If you are bitten, carefully and properly remove the tick, according to the guidelines set by your provincial health service. Save the tick in a sealed jar or in a zip-lock plastic bag, and take it to a health clinic in your area to be tested. (If pets are bitten, your veterinarian will have instructions for testing.) This will help determine if the tick is a carrier of disease.[1] — SN

Deer are eating *everything* in my garden. What can I do to stop them?

With three main wildlife corridors running right through the city of Calgary, our city residents have come to value our wildlife, including the deer. That is, until they find our gardens. After all, we are providing them with a rather sumptuous buffet. We can't resist a buffet, so why should they?

The short answer, unfortunately, is nothing much short of physical barriers will deter deer. If you are protecting individual beds and shrubs, then wire mesh encircling the bed or plants provides the best barrier. Do be prepared to move the barrier farther away from the shrubs or bed as the plants grow. If you wish to protect the entire garden, then 8-foot (2.5-metre) mesh or board fences are required. If you construct a mesh fence, then the mesh should be buried into the soil at the bottom, and if you go with a board fence, ensure the bottom board is flush with the soil level or slightly below ground to be effective. Deer are unlikely to leap into an area if they do not see a way to escape from it. Do pray that a moose doesn't come by, for it can charge right through the fence!

Adding shrubs of varying heights near the outside of the fence makes the barrier wider and makes it less possible for the deer to see into the garden and decide to jump over it. Creating a rock garden along the outside of the fence with varying heights and shapes of rocks will also deter deer as they will not have easy footing to navigate through the rocks.

You can try many commercial or homemade deterrents. However, they must be frequently changed as the deer will grow accustomed to them and will no longer perceive them to be a threat. This includes noisemakers, shiny or reflecting strips, and odours, such as the urine of predators.

There are also lists of plants guaranteed to be "deer proof" or "deer resistant" by whoever publishes them. The truth is that there is no plant safe from a deer if the deer fancies it or is truly hungry, and that includes prickly rose (*Rosa acicularis*). Generally, plants that are less likely to be on the buffet have fuzzy foliage such as that of lamb's ears (*Stachys byzantina*) or wormwood (*Artemisia* spp.); have thick leaves, like those of elephant's ears (*Bergenia* spp.) or irises (*Iris* spp.); have

Fences are your best bet to stop deer from chowing down on your plants.

prickles or thorns, such as those of globe thistles (*Echinops* spp.) or gooseberries (*Ribes uva-crispa*); are grasses like 'Karl Foerster' (*Calamagrostis* × *acutiflora* 'Karl Foerster'); are strongly scented like garlic; or are truly poisonous, like monkshood (*Aconitum napellus*) or daffodils (*Narcissus* spp.). Native plants often fare better than exotic species, as they have co-evolved with the deer.

Other than trying the above selections, there are only a couple of other options: Get a dog that lives outside in the garden and/or have a great sense of "live and let live."[2] —JM

Rabbits are dining on all my veggies! Is there anything I can do?

Just like deer, rabbits think that our vegetable beds are the best buffet in town. They especially like lettuces and other greens, though unlike a dog I know, they haven't been seen pulling out a carrot from the ground and munching on it!

Generally, raised beds above 1.5 feet (45 centimetres) deter rabbits as they usually won't jump into a bed. To be safe, a mesh fence of another 1.5 feet (45 centimetres) around the bed will keep everything protected within it.

I have also had some success with decoy plants, such as parsley, around the edges of the bed, where the rabbits can eat as much as they like and leave the more valuable crops alone.

Rabbits also become a nuisance in ornamental beds, where they view the flowering plants as dessert. As with deer, there are no really safe rabbit-proof plants. I have even had one eat a large tomato plant, which I hoped would give him a stomachache, seeing as the leaves contain toxins. Rabbits do not often follow the rules. They will generally—but not always—avoid fuzzy, thick, stinky, or prickly plants.

In winter, rabbits can cause damage to young trees and shrubs, eating the bark and twigs above snow level. Do wrap tree trunks with plastic guards and cover small shrubs with a well-anchored floating row cover as a deterrent to rabbits. —JM

Squirrels! What can be done about them digging up plants and bulbs?

Cute, but annoying!
(Photo courtesy of Rob Normandeau)

The eastern grey squirrel (*Sciurus carolinensis*)—you may also spot a black one in your garden, which has a mutation, allowing it to soak up the sun during cold winters—is a survivor. It is also non-native to the prairies. This is the squirrel that causes us the most hairpulling when it digs up our plants and bulbs in search of food.

Our native red squirrel (*Tamiasciurus hudsonicus*), on the other hand, cleans out green cones from atop our spruce trees, raining them down to the ground around our heads, but otherwise is a welcome visitor to our gardens.

I have long decided that there is no way to get the best of these grey or black squirrels. They are smart, inquisitive, and adaptable. They have a terrific sense of smell, and there are a lot of them.

They are also hungry, and with current dry conditions on the prairies reducing the numbers of nuts and seeds that they normally eat, they are seeking other sources of food, especially in the fall.

Instead, I protect newly planted seedlings, especially in containers, with barriers such as mesh covers until they fill out, and I make sure the soil in the container is well covered. My vegetable beds are covered with floating row covers to protect the plants from our intense sunlight and to keep whatever humidity is in the air around the plants and to provide moisture to the soil. The white floating covers also seem to deter the squirrels. Bulbs planted in the fall, when squirrels are most active in searching for food, are covered with chicken wire or flat stones. In the spring, when the bulbs have developed good root systems, they are safer from the squirrels, I hope.

Many gardeners will use deterrents such as blood meal, which has a pungent odour, or cayenne pepper, which is painful to the squirrels. Both these measures have downsides. Blood meal is primarily a fertilizer that is high in nitrogen. Too much nitrogen in the soil, and you get lots of quick growth that is weak, with few flowers. Cayenne pepper can be dangerous for birds or pets if it gets into their eyes. Commercial deterrents are available as well; however, all products must be constantly reapplied after a rainfall or watering.

Since squirrels are in the garden looking for food, it is wise to ensure that garbage bins are well sealed, and that no pet food is left out. Barbecue areas should be well cleaned. I do love feeding the birds that visit, so I have invested in baffles to deter the squirrels from getting at the feeders. They are not always successful, as these squirrels are motivated, but it does provide amusement value at times. Many people do feed squirrels, but I do not, and I am afraid that the blue jays no longer get their peanuts.

I also have three cats, and there is a dog next door. Their constant comings and goings are an effective deterrent as squirrels do view pets as a potential danger. Decoy owls and hawks, especially ones that move, are also effective.

Other than these measures, we must accept that squirrels are part of our garden environment and learn to live with them. A well-developed sense of humour helps too![3] —JM

How do I deal with skunks in my garden?

Skunks (*Mephitidae* spp.) are often viewed as unpleasant neighbours at best and, at worst, pests to be eliminated. Yet they are hugely beneficial to the ecosystem and your garden, in particular, as they eat mice, wasps, and other insects that are viewed as not being desirable. Which isn't to say that meeting up with a skunk in the dark is not a scary proposition as no one wants to be sprayed!

Skunks are usually only a temporary concern as they retreat to their dens in the spring to have their kits. Once the babies are ready to be on their own, moms and babies will be on their way. The trick to ensure that your garden doesn't become a maternity ward is to ensure that likely denning spaces are blocked or eliminated well before denning season. Spaces under decks are a prime spot as they are dark, dry, and quiet refuges away from predators. Skunks will also burrow under sheds and structures not flush to the soil and into woodpiles and any other loose stacks of materials. They may become stuck in window wells, so make sure that these inadvertent traps are covered. Eliminate food sources by keeping garbage bins sealed and compost piles turned. Feed pets indoors or remove outside food bowls nightly.

Should you discover a denning skunk in your garden, there are some options short of trapping and relocating the mother, which often results in the deaths of the kits and the mother skunk, as she is placed in an unfamiliar and likely unsafe environment. Skunks are nocturnal and non-aggressive on the whole, so a regime of mild harassment is in order to simply make your garden unpleasant for them. Playing a radio tuned to a talk station next to their hole, shining lights onto the opening, and setting substances with unpleasant smells, such as used kitty litter or citrus peels, nearby will encourage them to move along once the babies are born. Persistence is key as skunks are reluctant to leave nice homes. Keep the harassment going for a few days, then check to see if they are still at home by plugging up their den with straw or other soft materials. If the skunks are gone, it will stay undisturbed, but if the materials are moved aside, you'll know they are still there. Please avoid trying to block an entrance with permanent barriers when babies are still there as the mother skunk will be frantic to get to them.

The final option is to simply accept the presence of your friendly neighbourhood skunks finding a home in your garden, as I did one summer. Keep the lights on when going out at night and watch for them out and about. Skunks will only spray when they believe they are in danger of being dinner for a predator. They will give a warning of being scared if faced with a predator—usually a dog or us—by stamping their feet and growling. Simply back off, give them their space, and all will be well. After all, it is out of their back ends that their spray comes, released as a final resort, as they run for their lives!—JM

There are several humane options to discourage skunks from making your garden their home.

What can I do to stop raccoons from ravaging my garden?

These clever, ring-tailed mammals with the characteristic black "mask" coloura-tion over their eyes are not exactly welcome in most prairie gardens, but the truth is they are not going anywhere any time soon. Although we may consider them a nuisance, they nevertheless play a role in the ecosystem: They help to regulate populations of animals such as mice and voles, and they are excellent distributors (via droppings) of the seeds of the plants they have consumed.

Raccoons (*Procyon lotor*) are members of the Procyonidae family, which has only eighteen species in it, including kinkajous and coatis. Raccoons are typically two to three feet (sixty to ninety centimetres) long, and they weigh approximately 10 to 30 pounds (4.5 to 13.5 kilograms). They are omnivores, which means they'll eat everything from soup to nuts—literally. Favourite meals include fruits, berries, nuts, acorns, grain, insects, worms, fish, mice, rabbits, bird eggs, and cultivated crops, such as corn, melons, and squash. They'll even devour pickings from your compost pile. Every so often, they will also attack poultry. Raccoons are largely nocturnal, so they tend to feast in your yard while you're asleep in bed, but they will also emerge from their dens during the day if they require a snack.

In addition to having an extremely varied (and opportunistic) diet, raccoons have readily adapted to rural and urban areas, forests, marshes, and prairie grasslands. They can easily break into homes and other buildings to get at food sources. Raccoons move around frequently and don't stay in the same dens for long periods of time, except perhaps during the winter months. (Although they do not hibernate, they tend to become largely inactive during periods of severe weather.) They are also flexible at finding what constitutes a home: It can be anything from a hollow log to the crawl space beneath your deck.

A pregnant raccoon gives birth to two to three kits, usually around the month of May. The mother and the young stay together for up to a year; the father doesn't stick around to watch them grow up.

It is truly difficult to discourage a raccoon from your garden once it has decided to forage in it. Clean up all garbage, and ensure your garbage cans and compost bins have lids that cannot be opened by these dexterous creatures. If you can, store garbage cans in a building, such as a garage or shed. Bird feeders and their contents are huge attractants, so if raccoons are a constant issue, mount bird feeders on a free-standing pole instead of on or near a building or in a tree. If you have pet dogs, make sure their food dishes are not accessible to raccoons, or Fido will be surprised to find he has a new roommate hanging around his doghouse.

Remove all fruit litter or decomposing vegetables from the ground or raised beds. Harvest your produce as soon as it is ready to discourage unwanted taste tests.

If your raccoon troubles persist, you may have to call in a pest control company for help. They will live-trap and relocate the animal. This may be a temporary solution, however, as new raccoons may move in or the old one may come back. Male raccoons have ranges of up to eighteen miles (twenty-nine kilometres) in rural areas. Placing as many food sources out of reach as you can is the best option.[4]—SN

How can I deter porcupines from my yard?

*Porcupines can do significant
damage to your plants.*

North American porcupines (*Erethizon dorsatum*) are not aggressive animals, but the 30,000 barbed quills (actually modified hairs) they sport can prove injurious to dogs or other animals that get too close. (Porcupines cannot throw their quills, but they can slap their tails around to strike, and any creature that tries to take a bite or sniff—whether with curious or predatory intent—will get a muzzleful.)

Inhabitants of woodlands, porcupines will usually only enter human territory if food sources are scarce. As they do not hibernate and food is less available during colder weather, you'll notice their activity primarily during the winter months. They are mostly nocturnal, but you will sometimes see them ambling slowly about during the day. They have poor eyesight and don't spook easily—they know most creatures will avoid them.

Porcupines can cause significant damage to a garden, where they strip shrubs and young trees of bark and gnaw on branches and twigs. They particularly like wood, but they may not be able to resist your vegetable garden during the summer, and they also enjoy small fruits.

Porcupines may also scope out your property for potential den sites, particularly in the spring, in preparation for the birth of one to four offspring. They will look for crawl spaces under decks or openings in sheds or outbuildings.

Deterring porcupines from your yard may take a multipronged approach. Inspect and seal off all potential den sites, so that they won't be encouraged to establish their home sweet home. Ensure any pet food is stashed indoors. In the summer, set up motion-sensor water sprinklers near your vegetable garden and fruit bushes to try to scare them away. (Just don't forget about the locations of the sprinklers, or you and your family will end up getting a shower!)

Garden beds can be fenced off, but bear in mind that porcupines are excellent climbers and your design must thwart this ability. Some gardeners have had success with electric fences, but caution must be exercised with their use around children and pets.

Tree guards made of smooth sheets of aluminum will prevent climbing and the removal of bark and branches. Remember that the guards must be tall enough to accommodate the anticipated snow level during the winter, as the snow piles will allow porcupines to reach higher branches on the tree than during the summer. Porcupines tend to go after younger trees, leaving mature ones alone, so after a few years, the guards will no longer be needed.

If you are left with no other options and your local bylaws allow it, trapping and relocating porcupines may be the only solution. It is recommended to hire a pest control company to do the job, as it is difficult to entice these animals into a live trap, especially during the daytime. Use of a pole snare may be required.

If you do manage to accomplish the task yourself, move the porcupines to a site up to twenty-eight miles (forty-five kilometres) away. (Don't dump the animal on someone else's property or field, however.) Porcupines don't tend to travel long distances, so the same animal is not likely to return to your yard.

You may wonder what beneficial role this interesting but potentially pesky rodent plays in our ecosystem. Porcupines, like many other herbivores, are participants in the process of seed dispersal, which helps to ensure biodiversity.[5] — SN

Pocket gophers and voles: They are destroying my lawn and garden! How can they be stopped?

Often misidentified as moles, northern pocket gophers (*Thomomys talpoides*) are strong thick rodents named for their cheek pouches, which they use to carry food. These herbivores are not at all selective when it comes to chowing down on your garden—they'll pretty much eat anything with leaves. To add insult to injury, they are extremely adept at digging holes all over the place, as they design long elaborate burrows for nesting and shelter. You'll often see piles of loose soil near holes as they kick it up out of their burrow.

Unfortunately, controlling pocket gophers is difficult. They aren't likely to even bat an eyelash at poison bait traps if there are growing plants to chew on in the vicinity. Poison traps may work best in the fall or very early spring. (Of course, if using these types of traps, exercise caution if you have children or pets.) You can live-trap pocket gophers by digging into an active burrow and setting up box-style traps throughout. Check the traps several times a week, and be prepared to relocate the animals in an area where they won't harass other homeowners.[6]

Voles are another common rodent pest found in prairie gardens. Several species reside in this part of the country. You'll usually encounter the meadow vole (*Microtus pennsylvanicus*) and the prairie vole (*M. ochrogaster*). Voles resemble mice, but they are a bit stockier and possess rounder snouts and shorter, fur-covered tails. Like pocket gophers, they aren't discerning vegetarian diners. They can do a huge amount of damage to a vegetable garden in the summer and to young trees during the wintertime. One summer I checked one of my raised beds to find that voles had chewed into several of my growing zucchinis. There were neat lines of teeth marks across the skins. They had also dug into the soil beneath the bottom planks of the raised bed, hiding out in anticipation of their next veggie conquest.

Vole activity is most noticeable in the winter and spring, however. They tunnel just below the soil surface and hide under the snow cover to feed on roots and unprotected tree bark. In some cases, this can lead to girdling and the potential loss of trees. When the snow melts, the tracks and the damage to your lawn are highly visible.

Cutting your lawn short in the late autumn will prevent voles from hiding in the tall grass. Don't forget to collect the grass clippings! For the same reason, remove plant debris, such as dead leaves, fallen branches, and dropped fruit. Seal up or empty compost bins if you don't use them during the winter.

Plastic or wire mesh tree guards can protect young trees as long as you sink them into the ground at least six inches (fifteen centimetres) below the soil line. Anticipate the level of snowfall, and ensure the guards are tall enough to thwart voles that may climb on top of the snow piles to reach the exposed bark.

If you're not averse to killing voles, inexpensive snap-type mousetraps baited with peanut butter can be effective. Bear in mind that you may need lots of traps! (Again, monitor children and pets if you decide to go this route.)

If the population of pocket gophers or voles is too great to control, or you do not wish to look after the job yourself, hiring a pest control company is always a good solution.[7]—SN

How do I stop cats from digging and relieving themselves in the garden?

An option for dealing with cats in your garden is to create a special place for them to do their business. This may keep them out of the pea patch! (Photo courtesy of Tina Boisvert)

Although it is generally advised, especially in urban communities, that it is best for cats to live indoors, it is also understood that if you live in a rural area, cats are useful mousers on your property. And while you may keep your cats indoors, your neighbour may not, and the little felines may enjoy visiting your garden.

It's not easy to keep them from using your garden beds as a litter box. You may need to try several different tactics—probably many of them at the same time.

Mulching with river rock may help, as cats don't like to work to dig. Some gardeners use cones from coniferous trees, placing them on top of the soil. The cones are prickly and uncomfortable for cats to move around. You can also purchase plastic mats that have spikes on them, which you can lay on top of the soil. (The spikes aren't sharp and won't hurt the cats, but they will prevent them from walking on them. One problem with the mats, however, is they are not highly attractive.) If cats are climbing your fence to enter your yard, you can attach a raised wire along the top, along the full length of the yard, to prevent the cat from accessing your property. As an alternative, you can purchase plastic bird spikes, traditionally used to keep birds from landing in specific areas. Or you can plant low ground-cover conifers that are spiky and uncomfortable for cats to wander through.

Some gardeners swear by motion-sensor water sprinklers. Cats startle easily and most don't like water, so it is a solid, safe tactic.

Sometimes, offering up an actual area in your yard where cats can feel comfortable doing their business is a useful solution. Create a small space in a corner of your garden and fill it with sand to welcome kitties. (You could even frame the litter box with a planting of catmint or catnip to increase its appeal.) A huge drawback of this is that you'll have to regularly scoop the waste, an unpleasant task at best but worse if it's not even your cat creating it!

If you have a good rapport with your neighbours, approach the subject of their wandering cat with kindness and consideration. You might just solve the problem with a gentle word or two.

Finally, please don't use pepper-based products as a repellent for cats. It can severely irritate their eyes.[8] — SN

Strawberries are way too tantalizing to birds to leave uncovered.

Does coyote urine work to prevent pest animals from entering the garden? What about human urine?

It may be considered a bit gross, but using coyote urine—either in liquid or granular form—to deter pest critters, such as deer and rabbits, is at least a humane (and fairly inexpensive) method of control. The repellent may frighten "prey" animals due to its strong odour. The scent does not last for very long and frequent reapplication—especially of the liquid—is necessary, particularly during rainy weather. Bear in mind that pet dogs may find coyote urine extremely interesting. If you don't want them sniffing around the garden, you may want to avoid using the product.

The efficacy of using human urine as pest control is anecdotal, and we don't recommend its application in gardens. In addition, there may be health concerns associated with it.

How do I keep birds from eating the fruit in my garden?

Birds are wonderful creatures to encourage to spend time in your garden. Their presence increases the biodiversity of the landscape, and certain species provide functions such as consuming insect pests, acting as pollinators, and dispersing seeds. (Not only that, but many of them contribute amazing songs and beauty, and are a joy to watch!)

Sometimes, however—especially at harvest time—gardeners do not want to compete with birds for ripened bounty. We want that fruit for ourselves. There are several ways to prevent birds from stealing your harvest. Try a multipronged approach, and use more than one of these methods at the same time:

1. Site your fruit plants and vegetables away from nearby wooded areas where birds can live and hide. The close proximity makes it too easy for birds to dart out, grab fruit, then make a hasty escape. Eliminate this sense of security.
2. Tie streamers made of shiny metallic tape or ribbon to tree branches. (In garden plots, we've seen people put up mobiles made of discarded compact discs.) Foil whirligigs and other wind-driven, propeller-style deterrents mounted on tall poles are another option. The biggest issue with these types of flashing objects is that birds figure them out fairly quickly. You must move them on a regular basis.
3. Cover the plants. The canopies of short trees or entire shrubs may be wrapped in mesh bird netting and fastened with plant ties. The nets shouldn't fly off in a strong wind, but they must be easy for you to remove and replace when harvest time rolls around. One potential problem with bird netting is that the fruit closest to the edges of the nets can still be accessed by birds. Most of the yield will not be affected, however. Some gardeners are also concerned that the netting will trap birds. Prevent this by using nets with fine mesh. If you are growing small fruit, a hoop tunnel and a floating row cover (or stakes and a row cover for individual plants) are good alternatives to netting.—SN

Other Wacky, Weird, or Wonderful Things

5

I have liverworts and mosses growing in areas of my garden and I don't want them there. Is there anything I can do?

Bryophytes such as moss and liverworts are fascinating, non-vascular plants. (That means they don't have the same parts for uptake and transport of water and nutrients as other plants.) They are compact ground covers and spread slowly via spores. If part of your garden sits in the shade, is consistently damp, and has poor drainage with infertile compacted soil, you're likely to find moss and liverworts.

Truthfully, those kinds of conditions are not highly supportive of other types of plant life, so if you want the moss and liverworts out, you'll have to undertake some remediation work. Prune back overhanging trees and shrubs to give the location more sunlight and air circulation (and dry out the soil). Improve drainage by digging a trench, if feasible. Add compost to boost the soil's fertility.

Moss and liverworts can be removed by using a shovel. You won't have to dig too deeply—they don't have the same types of rooting systems as vascular plants. There may be a market for your freshly dug moss patches. Some gardeners deliberately cultivate moss gardens, and they might want to take the pieces off your hands. Check with gardening groups in your area to see if there is any interest before you dig.—SN

Moss and liverworts love damp, shady sites.

This crabapple is nearing the end of its lifespan and is covered in lichen.

There are mushrooms growing on the trunk of my tree. Is this bad? What can I do? What about lichens?

When you spot conks—often bracket or shelf mushrooms—on your trees, they are usually indicators that the tree's health is in decline. The spores of conks enter into tree wounds caused by bad pruning cuts, a mechanical injury such as a good whack with the weed trimmer, or frost cracks. The mushrooms grow out of the cracks, and as they do so, they introduce pathogens that cause rot in the tree. When the conks reproduce, they release thousands of spores, which are carried off by the wind to infect other wounded trees nearby. Conks usually infect older trees, as they are more likely to have suffered an injury than younger trees.

Lichens, on the other hand, are non-parasitic organisms made up of a unique combination of algae and fungi. Lichens themselves cannot harm trees, but they will grow on older trees or those that are no longer healthy.

There are no controls for conks and lichens. Lichens do not need to be treated or removed. Conks are a more serious issue and usually mean that the tree they are growing on has reached the end of its life. With the help of a certified arborist, assess the health of the tree, and determine if the removal should be done right away or if the tree is strong enough to continue standing for a while. The risk is that the weakened tree may fall in a storm and cause damage to property and human life. Cutting the conks off will not do anything other than improve the appearance of the tree, as the organisms will remain inside of the tree.

To help prevent conks from growing on your trees, prune carefully and do not leave stubs or create bad cuts. When using power equipment near trees, exercise caution so that the trees don't get nicked. Offer your trees a stress-free environment with sufficient moisture and nutrients for their individual needs. Site trees properly, and provide them with fertile soil with good texture and proper drainage. Trees that are happy will be less likely to contract problems such as conks.—SN

There are mushrooms growing in the mulch in my garden. Should I be concerned?

The appearance of mushrooms in mulch is definitely not a cause for concern.

No, it is great news!

Mushrooms are just the fruiting or reproductive bodies of fungi that are making their home in the mulch. When you use mulch in the garden, mushrooms are part of the environment you are cultivating. Most mushrooms that materialize out of mulch, almost like magic, after a rainy period are in woody materials, such as arborist wood chips, bark chips, or shredded bark, where there is a lot of carbon to break down. The job of fungi is to decompose the mulch over time and to allow it to contribute to the soil's texture and structure. Especially important in garden areas dominated by trees and shrubs, fungal-dominated soils contribute hugely to the health of the plants and overall growing environment.

On the other hand, you would not want to see mushrooms in mulch on beds devoted to annual plants—both edible and ornamental—as they prefer bacterially dominated soil. Seeing mushrooms in that mulch would mean that the soil has too many fungi to the detriment of bacterial populations, which would likely impact the way those plants are growing.

If you prefer not to have the mushrooms in the mulch, you can simply remove them by digging them out by hand or using a rake to break them up. Usually they will dry up when their spores are dispersed or when the weather turns hot and dry again.

The only caveat is to ensure that mulch is no deeper than two inches (five centimetres) at the most. Any deeper and the mulch can be a barrier to nesting and overwintering insects. It may also smother the underlying soil, causing anaerobic conditions that introduce a whole other set of problems affecting the health of the soil and the plants. We prefer to have mulch in our perennial beds be less than 3/4 inches (2 centimetres) with the occasional almost uncovered area. That depth gives all the benefits of mulch and provides habitat for soil-dwelling insects.

Please do not try to eat the mushrooms unless you are an expert. Many do contain toxins that are poisonous to humans and other mammals, to a greater or lesser extent.[1] —JM

A blobby goo just showed up in several places in my garden, primarily in the wood chips I have mulched my beds with. What is it and what can I do about it?

If it's yellow, light brown, pale pink, or creamy white and looks a bit like fluffy, foamy scrambled eggs, then what you've got is a slime mould that goes by the name *Fuligo septica* (scrambled egg slime mould or, more commonly, dog vomit slime mould). Dog vomit slime mould will typically reach a height of 1 3/4 inches (4.5 centimetres) and a spread of 8 inches (20 centimetres).[2]

Slime moulds are not mushrooms or any other type of fungus. They are related to single-celled organisms such as amoeba. There are approximately 700 species of slime moulds in the world, but dog vomit slime mould is the one you'll encounter most often in a prairie garden.

In the plasmodium stage of its life cycle, a slime mould crawls slowly over dead wood, decaying leaves, and decomposing mulch. They may be seriously ugly, but slime moulds play a large role in the consumption and breakdown of decaying organic matter. All of this feeding activity cycles back to the deposition of nutrients in the soil.

Slime moulds reproduce via spores—millions of spores![3] (In an interesting twist, they move to higher, drier, and sunnier ground to release them, as these conditions are more favourable for the job.)[4] The spores are carried by the wind.

Dog vomit slime mould is not edible. While it is not toxic to humans or pets, the floating spores may cause reactions in people who suffer from allergies. Otherwise, slime moulds aren't something to worry about, and they are actually quite fascinating. It is recommended to just let them do their thing. Slime moulds will usually vanish in a few days, but new ones may appear at a later date.

If you feel you must control a slime mould, you'll have your work cut out for you. Removing and replacing the mulch will not stop it; spores linger in the soil.

Every time you water, spores will be spread around. Completely drying out the affected area may assist somewhat. If you wish, you can scrape up as much of the active or dried mould as you can and dispose of it in the garbage. This will not remove all of the mould, but it may slow its progression into the spore-bearing phase. Cooler, drier weather will hinder its development (but not halt it); slime moulds thrive in hot, humid conditions, although they are adaptable to most worldwide climates. — SN

Is there anything that can be done to prevent poplar "fuzz"?

Poplar "fuzz" can exacerbate the troublesome symptoms of people who have severe pollen allergies. Another concern about it is the sheer messiness! It can even clog culverts, which can cause issues with water drainage.

The female trees produce the offensive abundance of cotton-like seeds, so the usual solution is to plant only male cultivars. Some selections to try in a prairie garden include 'Imperial' poplar (*Populus × canadensis* 'Imperial'), 'Assiniboine' poplar (*P.* × 'Assiniboine'), and 'Manitou' poplar (*P.* × 'Manitou').[5]—SN

*Female poplars produce
sneeze-inducing seeds.*

There is a large burl on a tree in my yard. What is it, and do I need to do something about it?

Burls are bumpy (and sometimes extremely large) growths on trees. They are usually caused by environmental injury, and sometimes by bacteria, fungi, or insect infestations. Occasionally, when a tree is harmed, the growth of the cambium goes into overdrive in order to protect the rest of the tree from the site of the injury. This excessive growth will result in the formation of a burl. The burls themselves will not harm the tree, except in extremely rare cases when they interfere with the tree's vascular system.

The treatment for burls is to just let them be. Cutting them out will wound the tree, leaving it vulnerable to attack by insects or diseases. Think of burls as interesting and unique additions to your landscape. — SN

There is no need to treat burl growth on trees.

There are a ton of spiders in my garden. Should I do anything about them?

These eight-legged arthropods make some people very nervous. The internet memes prescribing burning down the entire house if a single tiny spider is found inside circulate widely and garner understanding "likes" because spiders seem weird and unnatural and scary to many. The truth is, these fascinating creatures are actually one of the best pest control agents you'll ever find, and they perform those services for free!

Spiders are dedicated carnivores and do not eat plants. Ever. If you see them on your plants and think they're chowing down on the vegetation, they are likely eating the things that are eating your plants. (Or they are just hanging out enjoying the sun.) And while they do have venomous fangs and will bite if threatened, spiders do not deliberately attack humans. That's just not their nature. Aphids, on the other hand, are targets for spiders, as are mosquitoes, flies, caterpillars, and other pest insects. If you see a ton of spiders in your garden, chances are the site is overrun with these sorts of pests, and the spiders are taking care of business for you. It is true that spiders occasionally snag and eat bees and other beneficial insects, but one of their primary roles in the ecosystem is to dispose of abundant pests, which they do with gusto.

You'll find many species of spiders in your prairie garden; some of the most common include hunter spiders, such as the wolf (family Lycosidae), and the goldenrod crab (family Thomisidae), which has an ingenious method of camouflaging and changing its colour to match the flowers of the plants it hides upon. Jumping spiders such as the bold jumper (*Phidippus audax*) and the zebra jumper (*Salticus scenicus*) are also found in prairie gardens, as are web spinners, which include the rather sizable orb weavers, such as the cross orb weaver (*Araneus diadematus*).

Learn to respect and love—or at least cope with—the spiders in your garden. They are not there to cause any trouble, and they truly earn their keep.—SN

Something is creating large, perfectly circular holes in the leaves of my plants. What is doing this? Do I need to take action?

This haskap plant has been visited by leafcutter bees.

We always celebrate when we see those circular holes cut out of our rose leaves! It is confirmation that leafcutter bees are finding our gardens to be habitats to build their nests close by.

Leafcutter bees, and their close cousins mason bees, are solitary bees, part of the Megachilidae family, within the order Hymenoptera. Both types of bees construct nests for their young in holes and niches they find, such as hollow stems and old wood, with the leafcutter bees neatly cutting sections of leaves, rolling them to make cells, and inserting them into their nests. They then fill the cells with pollen and nectar, lay their eggs, and seal the ends. Typical nests have tubes with up to a dozen cells each.

We can provide habitat for these native species of the prairies by leaving old wood in our gardens. We also leave old delphinium, Joe Pye weed, lovage, and other pithy stalks and hollow perennial stems still standing from last year's garden to create extra habitat. You can also purchase premade nesting houses or make your own to provide habitat to attract even more of these types of bees to your garden.

As for the circular holes they create in our plants' foliage, we should consider them a badge of honour and do nothing. The rest of the leaf is still able to continue photosynthesizing, so the plants are not impacted at all. —JM

This might work if rabbits
could read . . .

Acknowledgements

Janet and Sheryl would like to thank:

Our fantastic publishing team at TouchWood Editions: Taryn Boyd (publisher), Kate Kennedy (editorial coordinator), Paula Marchese (copy editor), Tori Elliott (marketing and publicity coordinator), Tree Abraham (designer), Meg Yamamoto (proofreader), and Pat Touchie (owner). We'd also like to mention Renée Layberry, who worked with us in the early stages of the manuscript. We are appreciative of all of the support and encouragement we've received and we are delighted to work with such a wonderful group of people!

Thanks also to Rob Normandeau and Tina Boisvert, who generously contributed photographs to the book.

Janet is profoundly grateful to:

My co-author, Sheryl, for first approaching me with the idea that we could write a book together and then being such a fantastic and supportive writing partner!

My grandmother and mother for being such great gardeners themselves and assuming that of course I would follow in their footsteps. I think of both of them every day when I am in a garden!

My husband, Steve, my daughter, Jennifer, and son, David, for all the encouragement and support for my endeavours. Plus, their endless patience with me when my head is writing even when I am supposed to be paying attention to them!

All my friends who listen to me talk gardening year in and out and those special gardening friends who get down and dirty with me in gardening!

Sheryl sends out seriously big kudos to:

My co-author, Janet, who bestowed an immense and extremely valuable amount of knowledge, time, and effort on this project.

My husband, Rob, my mum and dad, my brother Derek, and the rest of my family and friends—for everything, really.

Notes

Chapter One

1. Chalker-Scott, "The Myth of Landscape Fabric," Washington State University; Garden Mentors (website), "Why Landscape Weed Barrier Is Ugly and Wasteful."

2. City of Edmonton, "Creeping Bellflower."

3. Oregon State University, "Horsetail."

4. Ohio State University, "Ohio Perennial and Biennial Weed Guide: Field Horsetail."

5. City of Calgary, "Dandelions."

6. Alberta Agriculture and Forestry, "Dandelion."

7. Bubar, McColl, and Hall, *Weeds of the Prairies*, 226–227; Reidy and Swanton, "Quackgrass," Ontario Ministry of Agriculture, Food and Rural Affairs; Montana State University, "Crabgrass vs. Quackgrass"; Connolly, "Quackgrass vs. Crabgrass," The Spruce (website).

8. Wheatland County, *Identification Guide for Alberta Invasive Plants*; Franklin County Noxious Weed Control Board, "Canada Thistle: Options for Control."

9. Government of Canada, "Re-evaluation Decision RVD 2018-13, Acetic Acid and Its Associated End-Use Products."

10. Health Canada, "Consumer Product Safety: Applications by Product."

Chapter Two

1. Sproule, "Aphids 101," Salisbury Greenhouse (website).

2. University of Missouri Integrated Pest Management, "Ants on Peony Flowers: An Example of Biological Mutualism"; Fry, Macaulay, and Williamson, *Garden Bugs of Alberta*, 168–170.

3. Hahn, Wold-Burkness, and Birlin, "Cutworms," University of Minnesota Extension.

4. Offin, "Tiny Asian Wasps Brought In to Fight Calgary's Invasive Lily Beetle," Global News; City of Calgary, "Red Lily Beetle."

5. Sproule, "Fungus Gnats," Salisbury Greenhouse (website).

6. Fry, Macaulay, and Williamson, *Garden Bugs of Alberta*, 74–75; Canola Council of Canada (website), "Canola Encyclopedia: Flea Beetles"; Bryant, "Flea Beetles: How to Identify and Get Rid of Flea Beetles," *The Old Farmer's Almanac* (website).

7. Allen, "Spittlebug: A Unique Little Insect," University of Connecticut Extension.

8. Harris, "How to Get Rid of Wasps Naturally," Mother Nature Network (website); Patterson, "8 Genius Ways to Get Rid of Wasps and Keep Them Away," Natural Living Ideas (website); Pests.org (website), "How to Get Rid of Wasps."

9. Bercha, "Bees," Insects of Alberta (website); Baresco, "Bumblebees of Alberta," Nature Alberta (website and PDF), 24–29; Scott, "Attract Pollinators to Your Garden!," Nature Alberta (website); Agriculture and Agri-Food Canada, "Native Pollinators and Agriculture in Canada."

10. Agriculture and Agri-Food Canada, "Leafhoppers."

11. Stevens, "Characteristics of Aster Yellows in Different Field Crops," Government of Saskatchewan.

12. Government of Alberta, *Backyard Pest Management in Alberta: Pests of Flowers.*

13. Pacific Northwest Insect Management Handbook, "Rose (Rosa)-Gall Wasp."

14. Bercha, "Woolly Oak Gall Wasps," Insects of Alberta (website).

15. Elmer, "Oak Gall Wasps," University of Texas at Austin Biodiversity Center.

16. Regional Municipality of Wood Buffalo, "Forest Tent Caterpillars"; Government of Canada, "Tent Caterpillars."

17. Bercha, "True Bugs," Insects of Alberta (website); Stink Bugs Guide (website), "Stink Bugs Guide"; Sproule, "Stink Bugs," Salisbury Greenhouse (website); Hueppelsheuser, "Brown Marmorated Stink Bug: A New Threat to Canadian Crops," Government of Alberta.

18. Agriculture and Agri-Food Canada, "Boxelder Bug"; City of Medicine Hat, "Boxelder Bugs: A Nuisance Pest."

19. City of Calgary, "Oystershell Scale"; Natural Resources Canada, "Oystershell Scale"; Hoover, "Oystershell Scale," Pennsylvania State University; CBC News, "Oystershell Scale Spreading through Calgary Hedges"; Fry, Macaulay, and Williamson, *Garden Bugs of Alberta*, 57; Bryan and Staal, *The Prairie Gardener's Book of Bugs*, 101.

20. BioForest, "What Is European Elm Scale?," *The Prairie Arborist.*

21. City of Calgary, "Elm Scale."

22. Skelly, "Horticultural Oils—What a Gardener Needs to Know," University of Nevada Cooperative Extension.

23. Agriculture and Agri-Food Canada, "Leafminers."

24. Bentley, "Leafrollers on Ornamental and Fruit Trees," University of California Agriculture and Natural Resources.

25. Ritcey and Chaput, "Onion Maggot Control," Ontario Ministry of Agriculture, Food, and Rural Affairs.

26. Government of Alberta, "Backyard Pests of Vegetables: Onion Maggot."

27. University of California Agriculture and Natural Resources, "Insectary Plants"; Hoffman, "Plants That Attract Beneficial Insects," Permaculture Research Institute (website).

Chapter Three

1. Government of Alberta, "Black Knot."

2. City of Calgary, "Bronze Leaf Disease"; Agriculture and Agri-Food Canada, "Bronze Leaf "; University of Manitoba, "Bronze Leaf Disease of Poplars."

3. Planet Natural Research Center (website), "Potato Scab"; Loria, "Vegetable Crops: Potato Scab," Cornell University.

4. Ontario Ministry of Agriculture, Food, and Rural Affairs, "Fire Blight."

5. Alberta Agriculture and Forestry, "Agri-Facts: Fireblight."

6. Missouri Botanical Garden (website), "Cedar-Apple Rust"; University of Manitoba, "Rusts"; ArborCare Tree Service (website), "Juniper-Hawthorn Rust"; Agrobase Canada (website), "Cedar Apple Rust"; The Morton Arboretum (website), "Cedar-Apple Rust."

7. Carroll, "Hollyhock Rust Treatment: How to Control Hollyhock Rust in the Garden," Gardening Know How (website); Missouri Botanical Garden (website), "Rust of Hollyhock"; Gould, "Plant Plagues: The Rusts Diseases," Rutgers University Plant and Pest Advisory.

8. Agriculture and Agri-Food Canada, "Cytospora Canker"; University of Illinois Extension, "Cytospora Canker of Poplars and Willows."

9. Barber, "Don't Lose Sight of What's Beneath the Soil," AgCanada.com (website); Canola Council of Canada (website), "Canola Encyclopedia: About Clubroot"; Rhoades, "Soft Rot Disease: How to Help Prevent Soft Rot Bacteria," Gardening Know How (website).

10. Timmerman and Korus, "Plant Pathogens," Science Education Resource Center, Carleton College; Isleib, "Signs and Symptoms of Plant Disease: Is It Fungal, Viral or Bacterial?," Michigan State University Extension; Small, "Plant Pathology," Colorado State University Extension.

Chapter Four

1. Centers for Disease Control and Prevention, "Preventing Ticks in the Yard."

2. Pearman and Pike, *Naturescape Alberta*, 155–156.

3. City of Calgary, "Tree Squirrels"; *The Old Farmer's Almanac* (website), "Squirrels: How to Identify and Get Rid of Squirrels in the Garden"; Pests.org (website), "How to Get Rid of Squirrels."

4. Rosatte, "Hinterland Who's Who: Raccoons," Canadian Wildlife Federation (website); Flynn, "More on Raccoons," Newport Bay Conservancy (website); Meyers, "Procyonidae," Animal Diversity Web (website); Havahart (website), "How to Keep Raccoons Out of Your Yard"; Havahart (website), "Raccoons"; British Columbia Conservation Foundation, "Raccoon," Wild Safe B.C. (website).

5. Bourne, "Agri-Facts: Control of Porcupine Damage," Alberta Agriculture, Food, and Rural Development.

6. Alberta Agriculture and Rural Development, "Agri-Facts: Control of Pocket Gophers and Ground Squirrels."

7. City of Calgary, "Voles."

8. Gervais, Luukinen, Buhl, and Stone, "Capsaicin," National Pesticide Information Center, Oregon State University Extension Services.

Chapter Five

1. Green, "How to Rid My Mulch of Mushrooms Growing in It," SFGate (website); Brantley, Davis, and Kuhns, "What Is Growing in My Landscape Mulch? Mushrooms, Slime Molds, and Fungus," Pennsylvania State University.

2. Missouri Department of Conservation, "Dog Vomit Slime Mold (Scrambled Egg Slime Mold)."

3. Klingaman, "Plant of the Week: Slime Mold, Dog Vomit," University of Arkansas System Cooperative Extension Service.

4. Henn, "The Plant Doctor: Slime Molds," Mississippi State University Extension.

5. North Dakota State University, "North Dakota Tree Handbook: Hybrid Poplar"; University of Saskatchewan, "Poplar Fuzz."

Sources

Agriculture and Agri-Food Canada. "Boxelder Bug." October 20, 2016. agr.gc.ca/eng /science-and-innovation/agricultural-practices/agroforestry/diseases-and-pests/boxelder -bug/?id=1198175203733.

———. "Bronze Leaf." August 7, 2015. agr.gc.ca/eng/science-and-innovation /agricultural-practices/agroforestry/diseases-and-pests/bronze-leaf/?id=1366999957779.

———. "Cytospora Canker." July 18, 2014. agr.gc.ca/eng/science-and -innovation/agricultural-practices/agroforestry/diseases-and-pests/cytospora -canker/?id=1367247436833.

———. "Leafhoppers." July 30, 2014. agr.gc.ca/eng/science-and-innovation /agricultural-practices/agroforestry/diseases-and-pests/leafhoppers/?id=1367260538110.

———. "Leafminers." August 10, 2015. agr.gc.ca/eng/science-and-innovation /agricultural-practices/agroforestry/diseases-and-pests/leafminers/?id=1367261204996.

———. "Native Pollinators and Agriculture in Canada." 2014. fs.fed.us/wildflowers /pollinators/documents/AgCanadaNativePollinators.pdf.

Agrobase Canada (website). "Cedar Apple Rust." Accessed June 14, 2019. agrobaseapp .com/canada/disease/cedar-apple-rust-1.

Alberta Agriculture and Forestry. "Agri-Facts: Fireblight." December 2016. www1.agric. gov.ab.ca/$department/deptdocs.nsf/all/agdex4149/$file/636-1.pdf.

———. "Dandelion." January 19, 2009. agric.gov.ab.ca/app107/display&id=122.

Alberta Agriculture and Rural Development. "Agri-Facts: Control of Pocket Gophers and Ground Squirrels." May 2008. www1.agric.gov.ab.ca/$department/deptdocs.nsf/all /agdex897/$file/684-1.pdf?OpenElement.

Allen, Joan. "Spittlebug: A Unique Little Insect." University of Connecticut Extension. July 24, 2017. bugs.uconn.edu/2017/07/24/spittlebug-a-unique-little-insect/#.

ArborCare Tree Service (website). "Juniper-Hawthorn Rust." Accessed June 14, 2019. arborcare.com/plant-management/disease/juniper-hawthorn-rust/.

Barber, Jennifer. "Don't Lose Sight of What's Beneath the Soil." AgCanada.com. January 26, 2018. agcanada.com/gfm_spons_content/dont-lose-sight-of-whats-beneath -the-soil.

Baresco, Dennis. "Bumblebees of Alberta." Nature Alberta (website and PDF). Summer 2012. naturealberta.ca/wp-content/uploads/2013/02/NA-Summer-2012 -LOW-1.pdf.

Bentley, W.J. "Leafrollers on Ornamental and Fruit Trees." University of California Agriculture and Natural Resources. Accessed June 14, 2019. ipm.ucanr.edu/PMG /PESTNOTES/pn7473.html.

Bercha, R. "Bees." Insects of Alberta (website). Accessed June 13, 2019. insectsofalberta.com/bees.htm.

———. "True Bugs." Insects of Alberta (website). Accessed June 14, 2019.

insectsofalberta.com/truebugs.htm.

———. "Woolly Oak Gall Wasps." Insects of Alberta (website). Accessed June 13, 2019. insectsofalberta.com/woolyoakgallwasp.htm.

BioForest. "What Is European Elm Scale?" *The Prairie Arborist*, no. 2 (2017): 4. isaprairie.com/wp-content/uploads/2014/01/PR-ARB-Issue-2-2017.pdf.

Bourne, John. "Agri-Facts: Control of Porcupine Damage." Alberta Agriculture, Food, and Rural Development. July 2005. www1.agric.gov.ab.ca/$department/deptdocs.nsf /all/agdex3470/$file/684-11.pdf?OpenElement.

Brantley, Elizabeth A., Donald D. Davis, and Larry J. Kuhns. "What Is Growing in My Landscape Mulch? Mushrooms, Slime Molds, and Fungus." Pennsylvania State University. January 1, 1997. extension.psu.edu/what-is-growing-in-my-landscape-mulch -mushrooms-slime-molds-and-fungus.

British Columbia Conservation Foundation. "Raccoon." Wild Safe B.C. (website). Accessed June 14, 2019. wildsafebc.com/raccoon/.

Bryan, Nora, and Ruth Staal. *The Prairie Gardener's Book of Bugs*. Ontario: Fitzhenry & Whiteside, 2003.

Bryant, Greg. "Flea Beetles: How to Identify and Get Rid of Flea Beetles." *The Old Farmer's Almanac* (website). almanac.com/pest/flea-beetles.

Bubar, Carol J., Susan J. McColl, and Linda M. Hall. *Weeds of the Prairies*. Edmonton: Alberta Agriculture and Forestry, 2000. archive.org/details/weedsofprairies00buba

Canola Council of Canada (website). "Canola Encyclopedia: About Clubroot." April 23, 2019. canolacouncil.org/canola-encyclopedia/diseases/clubroot/about-clubroot/.

———. "Canola Encyclopedia: Flea Beetles." June 10, 2019. canolacouncil.org /canola-encyclopedia/insects/flea-beetles/.

Carroll, Jackie. "Hollyhock Rust Treatment: How to Control Hollyhock Rust in the Garden." Gardening Know How (website). April 4, 2018. gardeningknowhow.com /ornamental/flowers/hollyhock/hollyhock-rust-in-gardens.htm.

CBC News. "Oystershell Scale Spreading through Calgary Hedges." May 27, 2015. cbc .ca/news/canada/calgary/oystershell-scale-spreading-through-calgary-hedges-1.3089264.

Centers for Disease Control and Prevention. "Preventing Ticks in the Yard." February 22, 2019. cdc.gov/ticks/avoid/in_the_yard.html.

Chalker-Scott, Linda. "The Myth of Landscape Fabric." Washington State University. Accessed June 12, 2019. s3.wp.wsu.edu/uploads/sites/403/2015/03/landscape-fabric.pdf.

City of Calgary. "Bronze Leaf Disease." Accessed June 14, 2019. calgary.ca/CSPS/Parks /Pages/Planning-and-Operations/Pest-Management/Bronze-leaf-disease-(BLD).aspx.

———. "Dandelions." Accessed June 12, 2019. calgary.ca/CSPS/Parks/Pages/Planning -and-Operations/Pest-Management/Dandelions.aspx.

———. "Elm Scale." Accessed June 14, 2019. calgary.ca/CSPS/Parks/Pages/Planning -and-Operations/Pest-Management/Elm-scale.aspx.

———. "Oystershell Scale." Accessed June 14, 2019. calgary.ca/CSPS/Parks/Pages

/Planning-and-Operations/Pest-Management/Oystershell-Scale.aspx.

————. "Red Lily Beetle." Accessed June 13, 2019. calgary.ca/CSPS/Parks/Pages /Planning-and-Operations/Pest-Management/Red-lily-beetle.aspx.

————. "Tree Squirrels." Accessed June 14, 2019. calgary.ca/CSPS/Parks/Pages /Planning-and-Operations/Pest-Management/Tree-squirrels.aspx.

————. "Voles." Accessed June 14, 2019. calgary.ca/CSPS/Parks/Pages/Planning-and -Operations/Pest-Management/Voles.aspx.

City of Edmonton. "Creeping Bellflower." Accessed June 12, 2019. edmonton.ca /programs_services/pests/creeping-bellflower.aspx.

City of Medicine Hat. "Boxelder Bugs: A Nuisance Pest." Accessed June 14, 2019. medicinehat.ca/government/departments/parks-and-recreation/pest-management /animals-insects/boxelder-bugs.

Connolly, Kathleen. "Quackgrass vs. Crabgrass." The Spruce (website). February 15, 2019. thespruce.com/quackgrass-crabgrass-easily-confused-lawn-weeds-2153114.

Elmer, Nicole L. "Oak Gall Wasps." University of Texas at Austin Biodiversity Center. October 31, 2018. biodiversity.utexas.edu/news/entry/oak-gall-wasps.

Flynn, Rosemary. "More on Raccoons." Newport Bay Conservancy (website). June 2006. newportbay.org/wildlife/mammals/more-on-raccoons/.

Franklin County Noxious Weed Control Board. "Canada Thistle: Options for Control." Accessed June 12, 2019. nwcb.wa.gov/images/weeds/Canada-thistle_Franklin.pdf.

Fry, Ken, Doug Macaulay, and Don Williamson. *Garden Bugs of Alberta: Gardening to Attract, Repel and Control*. Edmonton: Lone Pine Publishing, 2008.

Garden Mentors (website). "Why Landscape Weed Barrier Is Ugly and Wasteful." September 26, 2012. gardenmentors.com/garden-help/gardening-guidelines/why -landscape-fabric-weed-barrier-wasteful/.

Gervais, J.A., B. Luukinen, K. Buhl, and D. Stone. "Capsaicin." National Pesticide Information Center, Oregon State University Extension Services. March 2009. npic .orst.edu/factsheets/capgen.html.

Gould, Ann. "Plant Plagues: The Rusts Diseases." Rutgers University Plant and Pest Advisory. May 18, 2015. plant-pest-advisory.rutgers.edu/plant-plagues-the-rusts-diseases/.

Government of Alberta. *Backyard Pest Management in Alberta: Pests of Flowers*. 2014. www1.agric.gov.ab.ca/$Department/deptdocs.nsf/all/ipd14865/$FILE /BackyardPestMgmt_flowers.pdf.

————. "Backyard Pests of Vegetables: Onion Maggot." 2014. www1.agric.gov.ab .ca/$Department/deptdocs.nsf/all/ipd14865/$FILE/BackyardPestMgmt_vegetables.pdf.

————. "Black Knot." Accessed June 14, 2019. alberta.ca/black-knot.aspx.

Government of Canada. "Re-evaluation Decision RVD 2018-13, Acetic Acid and Its Associated End-Use Products." May 15, 2018. canada.ca/en/health-canada/services /consumer-product-safety/reports-publications/pesticides-pest-management/decisions -updates/reevaluation-decision/2018/acetic-acid.html.

————. "Tent Caterpillars." June 4, 2013. canada.ca/en/health-canada/services/pest -control-tips/tent-caterpillars.html.

Green, Jenny. "How to Rid My Mulch of Mushrooms Growing in It." SFGate (website), December 14, 2018. homeguides.sfgate.com/rid-mulch-mushrooms -growing-93511.html.

Hahn, Jeffrey, Suzanne Wold-Burkness, and Beth Birlin. "Cutworms." University of Minnesota Extension. 2018. extension.umn.edu/yard-and-garden-insects/cutworms.

Harris, Kimi. "How to Get Rid of Wasps Naturally." Mother Nature Network (website). June 27, 2013. mnn.com/your-home/at-home/blogs/how-to-get-rid-of-wasps-naturally.

Havahart (website). "How to Keep Raccoons Out of Your Yard." Accessed June 14, 2019. havahart.com/articles/raccoons-yard.

————. "Raccoons." Accessed June 14, 2019. havahart.com/raccoon-facts.

Health Canada. "Consumer Product Safety: Applications by Product." June 13, 2019. pr-rp.hc-sc.gc.ca/pi-ip/result-eng.php?1=0&2=501&3=pr&4=n&5=1&6=ASC&7=R& 8=E.

Henn, Alan, Dr. "The Plant Doctor: Slime Molds." Mississippi State University Extension. extension.msstate.edu/publications/the-plant-doctor-slime-molds.

Hoffman, Fred. "Plants That Attract Beneficial Insects." Permaculture Research Institute (website). October 4, 2014. permaculturenews.org/2014/10/04/plants-attract -beneficial-insects/.

Hoover, Greg. "Oystershell Scale." Pennsylvania State University. November 2003. ento.psu.edu/extension/factsheets/oystershell-scale.

Hueppelsheuser, Tracy. "Brown Marmorated Stink Bug: A New Threat to Canadian Crops." Government of Alberta. February 2013. agric.gov.ab.ca/crops/hort/bv2013 /bmsb-alberta.pdf.

Isleib, Jim. "Signs and Symptoms of Plant Disease: Is It Fungal, Viral or Bacterial?" Michigan State University Extension. December 19, 2012. canr.msu.edu/news/signs _and_symptoms_of_plant_disease_is_it_fungal_viral_or_bacterial.

Klingaman, Gerald. "Plant of the Week: Slime Mold, Dog Vomit." University of Arkansas System Cooperative Extension Service. August 25, 2006. uaex.edu/yard -garden/resource-library/plant-week/mold-slime-8-25-06.aspx.

Loria, Rosemary. "Vegetable Crops: Potato Scab." Cornell University. October 1991. vegetablemdonline.ppath.cornell.edu/factsheets/Potato_Scab.htm.

Meyers, Phil. "Procyonidae." Animal Diversity Web (website). 2000. animaldiversity .org/accounts/Procyonidae/.

Missouri Botanical Garden (website). "Cedar-Apple Rust." Accessed June 14, 2019. missouribotanicalgarden.org/gardens-gardening/your-garden/help-for-the-home -gardener/advice-tips-resources/pests-and-problems/diseases/rusts/cedar-apple-rust.aspx.

————. "Rust of Hollyhock." Accessed June 14, 2019. missouribotanicalgarden.org /gardens-gardening/your-garden/help-for-the-home-gardener/advice-tips-resources/pests -and-problems/diseases/rusts/rust-of-hollyhock.aspx.

Missouri Department of Conservation. "Dog Vomit Slime Mold (Scrambled Egg Slime Mold)." Accessed June 14, 2019. nature.mdc.mo.gov/discover-nature/field-guide/dog -vomit-slime-mold-scrambled-egg-slime-mold.

Montana State University. "Crabgrass vs. Quackgrass." April 13, 2018. msuextension .org/broadwater/blog-article.html?id=17622.

The Morton Arboretum (website). "Cedar-Apple Rust." Accessed June 14, 2019. mortonarb.org/trees-plants/tree-and-plant-advice/help-diseases/cedar-apple-rust.

Natural Resources Canada. "Oystershell Scale." August 4, 2015. tidcf.nrcan.gc.ca/en /insects/factsheet/5963.

North Dakota State University. "North Dakota Tree Handbook: Hybrid Poplar." Accessed June 14, 2019. ag.ndsu.edu/trees/handbook/th-3-133.pdf.

Offin, Sarah. "Tiny Asian Wasps Brought In to Fight Calgary's Invasive Lily Beetle." Global News. August 9, 2016. globalnews.ca/news/2874158/tiny-asian-wasps-brought-in -to-fight-calgarys-invasive-lily-beetle/.

Ohio State University. "Ohio Perennial and Biennial Weed Guide: Field Horsetail." Accessed June 12, 2019. oardc.ohio-state.edu/weedguide/single_weed.php?id=56.

The Old Farmer's Almanac (website). "Squirrels: How to Identify and Get Rid of Squirrels in the Garden." Accessed June 14, 2019. almanac.com/pest/squirrels.

Ontario Ministry of Agriculture, Food, and Rural Affairs. "Fire Blight." July 21, 2011. omafra.gov.on.ca/english/crops/facts/fireblight.htm.

Oregon State University. "Horsetail." Accessed June 12, 2019. oregonstate.edu/dept /nursery-weeds/weedspeciespage/horsetail/Equisetum_arvense_horsetail.html.

Pacific Northwest Insect Management Handbook. "Rose (Rosa)-Gall Wasp." Accessed June 13, 2019. pnwhandbooks.org/node/7043/print.

Patterson, Susan. "8 Genius Ways to Get Rid of Wasps and Keep Them Away." Natural Living Ideas (website). March 29, 2017. naturallivingideas.com/get-rid-of-wasps/.

Pearman, Myrna, and Ted Pike. Naturescape Alberta: Creating and Caring for Wildlife Habitat at Home. Red Deer: Red Deer River Naturalists and Federation of Alberta Naturalists, 2000.

Pests.org (website). "How to Get Rid of Squirrels." 2019. pests.org/how-to-get-rid-of -squirrels/.

———. "How to Get Rid of Wasps." 2019. pests.org/get-rid-of-wasps/.

Planet Natural Research Center (website). "Potato Scab." Accessed June 14, 2019. planetnatural.com/pest-problem-solver/plant-disease/potato-scab/.

Regional Municipality of Wood Buffalo. "Forest Tent Caterpillars." Accessed June 13, 2019. rmwb.ca/Municipal-Government/municipal_departments/Public-Operations /Parks---Trails/Caring-for-our-trees/Forest-Tent-Caterpillars.htm.

Reidy, M.E., and C.J. Swanton. "Quackgrass." Ontario Ministry of Agriculture, Food and Rural Affairs. June 1, 1993. omafra.gov.on.ca/english/crops/facts/quackgrass.htm.

Rhoades, Jackie. "Soft Rot Disease: How to Help Prevent Soft Rot Bacteria." Gardening

Know How (website). April 5, 2018. gardeningknowhow.com/plant-problems/disease/bacterial-soft-rot.htm.

Ritcey, Gwen, and Jim Chaput. "Onion Maggot Control." Ontario Ministry of Agriculture, Food, and Rural Affairs. July 1998. omafra.gov.on.ca/english/crops/facts/00-017.htm.

Rosatte, Richard. "Hinterland Who's Who: Raccoons." Canadian Wildlife Federation (website). 2008. hww.ca/en/wildlife/mammals/raccoon.html.

Scott, Blair. "Attract Pollinators to Your Garden!" Nature Alberta (website). April 21, 2016. naturecanada.ca/news/blog/attract-pollinators-to-your-garden/.

Skelly, JoAnne. "Horticultural Oils—What a Gardener Needs to Know." University of Nevada Cooperative Extension. 2013. unce.unr.edu/publications/files/ho/2013/fs1320.pdf.

Small, Mary. "Plant Pathology." Colorado State University Extension. November 2017. cmg.extension.colostate.edu/Gardennotes/331.pdf.

Sproule, Rob. "Aphids 101." Salisbury Greenhouse (website). Accessed June 13, 2019. salisburygreenhouse.com/aphids-101/.

———. "Fungus Gnats." Salisbury Greenhouse (website). Accessed June 13, 2019, salisburygreenhouse.com/fungus-gnats/.

———. "Stink Bugs." Salisbury Greenhouse (website). Accessed June 14, 2019. salisburygreenhouse.com/stink-bugs/.

Stevens, Danielle. "Characteristics of Aster Yellows in Different Field Crops." Government of Saskatchewan. Accessed August 21, 2019. https://www.saskatchewan.ca/business/agriculture-natural-resources-and-industry/agribusiness-farmers-and-ranchers/sask-ag-now/crops/crop-production-news/cpn-archives/crop-production-news—2016-issues/crop-production-news-2016-issue-5/aster-yellows.

Stink Bugs Guide (website). "Stink Bugs Guide." Accessed June 14, 2019. stinkbugsguide.net/.

Timmerman, A.D., and K.A. Korus. "Plant Pathogens." Science Education Resource Center, Carleton College. 2014. serc.carleton.edu/integrate/teaching_materials/food_supply/student_materials/1230.

University of California Agriculture and Natural Resources. "Insectary Plants." Accessed June 14, 2019. ipm.ucanr.edu/mitigation/insectary_plants.html.

University of Illinois Extension. "Cytospora Canker of Poplars and Willows." May 1990. ipm.illinois.edu/diseases/series600/rpd661/index.html.

University of Manitoba. "Bronze Leaf Disease of Poplars." Accessed June 14, 2019. umanitoba.ca/faculties/afs/hort_inquiries/725.html.

———. "Rusts." Accessed June 14, 2019. umanitoba.ca/faculties/afs/hort_inquiries/748.html.

University of Missouri Integrated Pest Management. "Ants on Peony Flowers: An Example of Biological Mutualism." May 29, 2018. ipm.missouri.edu/MEG/2018/5/antsOnPeonies/.

University of Saskatchewan. "Poplar Fuzz." February 2, 2018. gardening.usask.ca /articles-disorders/poplar-fuzz.php.

Wheatland County. *Identification Guide for Alberta Invasive Plants*. Accessed June 12, 2019. edmonton.ca/documents/PDF/Weed_Identification_Book.pdf.

Index

Page numbers in italics refer to photographs.

hollyhock rust, 89
  powdery mildew, 77
fungicide, 33, 87
fungus gnat, 38

G
gall
  black knot, 78
  bullet gall, 54–55
  cedar-apple rust, 86
  cedar-hawthorn rust, 86
  cedar-quince rust, 86
  cynipid, 54–55
  mossy rose gall, 54–55
  woolly oak gall, 54–55
garlic, 58, 100
garlic spray, 58, 93
girdling, 12, 84, 110
golden marguerite, 73
goldenrod, 73
gooseberry, 100
grapevine, 52
grass, 'Karl Foerster', 100
grass clippings, 14
gypsum, 83

H
hand-pulling, 16, 19
haskap, *129*
hawthorn, 61, 84, 86
herbicide, 24, 33
  selective, 16
hollyhock rust, 88
horsetail. *See* field horsetail
horticultural oil, 61, 65–66, 69
  active ingredient, 66
  soilborne disease, 93
hosta, 96
hoverfly, 72

I
insect, 28–73, 46, 127
  beneficial, 8, 46, 53, 67, 128
  pollinators, 8, 32, 46, 72
  scale, 66
  See also specific insects
insectary plants, 72–73
insecticidal soap, 53, 55, 66

insecticide, 33
  systemic, 65
Integrated Pest Management, 8–9
  ants, 29
  bronze leaf disease, 80
  interplanting, 40, 43, 72
  IPM. *See* Integrated Pest Management
iris, 99

J
Japanese tree lilac, 92
Joe Pye weed, 129
juniper, 86

K
kale, 42
kaolin clay, 58

L
lacewing, 72
ladybug, 7, 29, 53, 72
lamb's ears, 73, 99
landscape fabric, 12–14
larch, 89
larkspur, 39
  Nuttall's, 39
  tall, 39
lavender, 43, 73
lawn, 19–21, 98, 111
  ants, 30
leafhopper, 52–53, 66
  aster yellows, vectors for, 52
leafminer, 66–67, 67
  birch, 66
  cocoon, 67
leafroller moth, 68, 69
  birds as control, 69
  horticultural oil as control, 69
  parasitoid wasps as control, 69
leaf spot, 66
lemon balm, 73
lettuce, 101
lichen, *120*, 121
lilac, 61
liverwort, 118, *119*
  spores, 118
live-trap, 107, 109–110
lovage, 73, 129

About the Authors

SHERYL NORMANDEAU was born and raised in the Peace Country region of northern Alberta and has made Calgary her home since 1994. A writer and master gardener, Sheryl holds a bachelor's degree in English, as well as a Prairie Horticulture Certificate and an Urban Sustainable Agriculture Certificate. Since 2013, she has served as the online Ask an Expert for the Calgary Horticultural Society. She works at the Calgary Public Library—besides gardening, books of all kinds are her grand passion! She is a small-space gardener (on a tiny balcony and in a plot in a nearby community garden) and she is most enthusiastic about growing veggies. She lives with her husband, Rob, their rescue cat, Smudge, and a tankful of freshwater fish. Find Sheryl at Flowery Prose (floweryprose.com), on Facebook (@FloweryProse), Twitter (@Flowery_Prose), and Instagram (flowery_prose).

JANET MELROSE was born in Trinidad, West Indies, and immigrated to Canada in 1964. She has lived in Calgary since 1969. She is a master gardener and the creator and owner of the successful horticulture business Calgary's Cottage Gardener, which specializes in garden education, horticultural therapy, and advocating for sustainable local food systems. She holds bachelor's degrees in sociology and history, a Prairie Horticulture Certificate, and a Horticultural Therapy Certificate. Janet is a lifelong gardener, coming from a heritage of English gardening. She has a large garden at home in the suburbs of Calgary that can only be described as a typical cottage garden. She cares for eight other gardens throughout Calgary through her work as a horticultural therapist, as well as a bed at the Inglewood Community Garden. She is married to Steve and has two children, Jennifer and David. Three cats, Patrick, Theo, and Mia, currently own their home and patrol against the deer, hares, squirrels, skunk, mice, and assorted birds that believe the garden is theirs, too! Connect with Janet on Facebook (@Calgarys-Cottage-Gardener), Twitter (@CalCottageGrdnr), and Instagram (CalgarysCottageGardener).

NOTES

NOTES

NOTES

NOTES

NOTES

NOTES

About the Series

It looks like you've discovered the **Guides for the Prairie Gardener.** This budding series puts the combined knowledge of two lifelong prairie gardeners at your grubby fingertips. Whether you've just cleared a few square feet for your first bed of veggies or are a seasoned green thumb stumped by that one cultivar you can't seem to master, we think you'll find Janet and Sheryl the ideal teachers. Find answers on seeds, soil, trees, flowers, weather, climate, pests, pots, and quite a few more. These slim but mighty volumes, handsomely designed, make great companions at the height of summer in the garden trenches and during cold winter days planning the next season. With regional expertise, elegance, and a sense of humour, Janet and Sheryl take your questions and turn them into prairie gardening inspiration. For more information, and for other titles in the series, visit touchwoodeditions.com/guidesprairiegardener.